Exercises in Media Writing

Exercises in Media Writing

Vincent F. Filak

University of Wisconsin–Oshkosh

FOR INFORMATION:

CQ Press
An Imprint of SAGE Publications, Inc.
2455 Teller Road
Thousand Oaks, California 91320
E-mail: order@sagepub.com

SAGE Publications Ltd.
1 Oliver's Yard
55 City Road
London EC1Y 1SP
United Kingdom

SAGE Publications India Pvt. Ltd.
B 1/I 1 Mohan Cooperative Industrial Area
Mathura Road, New Delhi 110 044
India

SAGE Publications Asia-Pacific Pte. Ltd.
3 Church Street
#10-04 Samsung Hub
Singapore 049483

Acquisitions Editor: Terri Accomazzo
Production Editor: Bennie Clark Allen
Editorial Assistant: Sarah Wilson
Copy Editor: Jim Kelly
Typesetter: C&M Digitals (P) Ltd.
Proofreader: Jen Grubba
Cover Designer: Scott Van Atta
Marketing Manager: Jillian Ragusa

Printed in the United States of America

Library of Congress Cataloging-in-Publication Data

Names: Filak, Vincent F. author.

Title: Exercises in media writing / Vincent F. Filak.

Description: Los Angeles : CQ Press, [2018]

Identifiers: LCCN 2018006754 | ISBN 9781544338101 (pbk. : alk. paper)

Subjects: LCSH: Mass media—Authorship.

Classification: LCC P96.A86 F5525 2018 | DDC 808.06/6302—dc23
LC record available at https://lccn.loc.gov/2018006754

This book is printed on acid-free paper.

18 19 20 21 22 10 9 8 7 6 5 4 3 2 1

CONTENTS

CONTENTS

AUDIENCE-CENTRIC MEDIA

REVIEW

1. What is an audience-centric approach to media? How is it similar to and different from previous approaches media outlets took with regard to publishing content? *It focuses on what the audience wants to hear and what will grab their attention. Certain information will be put on specific platforms based on what demographic is to be reached.*

2. What are three types of information media professionals need to gather to create audience segmentation? Define and differentiate among these three forms of information.

3. What is the difference between a "platform" and an "outlet"?

4. What does it mean to "personify" an audience? How does it work and how does it benefit you as a media writer?

5. What do the letters in the acronym "FOCII" stand for, and what does "FOCII" mean overall as a concept?

6. What are the two key questions the book tells you to ask of yourself to ensure you are approaching your work in an audience-centric way?

WRITING EXERCISES

1. Choose a media outlet you rely on for information and select five pieces of content (stories, blog posts, etc.) that appeal to you. Then, apply the FOCII elements to them. Which interest elements are most prevalent? Which ones are missing or rarely used? Write a short essay that outlines what made these pieces appeal to you and the degree to which the interest elements played a role in your selections. Also, outline what makes these pieces similar and what makes them different in terms of what they tell you and why you care about them.

2. Read each of the following sentences below and then explain which interest elements most directly apply to it and why:
    *   President Donald Trump signed an agreement with Russia that will leave both countries with no nuclear weapons by 2040.
    *   The Board of Trustees at your school announced last week that it will increase tuition by 10 percent next year, despite your school president's specific request to cut tuition costs.
    *   Officials at your university have announced that a rare form of bacterial meningitis has struck four students in the largest residence hall on your campus.
    *   The governor of your state has just been impeached because of an arcane provision in the state's constitution that requires all politicians to weigh less than 300 pounds.

3. Select one source of information you found to be dominating your media diet and examine it for the three things the book says that journalists "owe" their audience: accuracy, value and fairness/objectivity. How well do you think this source does in meeting those standards? In what areas does the source excel, and where could it do a better job for its readers or viewers?

4. Pick a publication that has the potential to see an audience change over time, such as a teen magazine or a parenting publication. Find one of the oldest issues of that publication easily available to you, either online or in your library's archives, as well as the most recent issue. Examine the publication for things that remain constant over time, in terms of content, images, themes and so forth. Also, assess what things have changed over the time span the two issues cover. Write a short analytical essay that explains the similarities and differences as well as why you think the publication has remained the same and yet changed over time.

5. Find a press release on a topic associated with your school. It can be about anything, from a budget crisis to an upcoming event. Now, find a news report on that same topic. It can be from the student newspaper, a city newspaper, a local blog, a television report or any other "news-centric" media outlet. In a short essay, outline the key elements featured in the release and the news report. Then compare and contrast the two pieces in terms of the interest elements they feature and the key needs listed in the chapter. Finally, explain which piece was more valuable to you as a reader and why.

6. Review a week's worth of content from a local media outlet (newspaper, website, TV station, etc.), and keep track of the topics they cover and which kinds of news get the most attention. Review your notes and write a short paper that explains your findings and whether you think the coverage reflects the interests of the audience of the media outlet.

BEING ACCURATE, RELYING ON THE FACTS

REVIEW

1. What does the term "gatekeeping" mean, and how does it relate to the role of media professionals?

2. List some of the ways in which "fake news" can be defined. What are some ways you can avoid getting faked out when it comes to potentially false content?

3. What are some of the processes you should conduct in a basic fact check?

4. What is the difference between a primary and a secondary source?

5. What does the line "If your mother says she loves you, go check it out" mean in the context of fact checking?

WRITING EXERCISES

1. Below is a list of 10 "facts" that might or might not be true. Determine if they are true or false through research, and include a source for each fact. If you find it to be false, explain why this is the case and cite your source.

    a. On Dec. 19, 1998, the House of Representatives impeached President Bill Clinton, making him the first president to be impeached since Richard Nixon.

    b. Children in the early 1900s who got lead poisoning often contracted the illness from the tips of their pencils.

    c. During the trial for the shooting death of San Francisco politicians George Moscone and Harvey Milk, Dan White's legal team coined the "Twinkie defense," arguing that White's judgment had been impaired by a heavy consumption of junk food.

    d. Singer Ozzy Osbourne bit the head off a bat while in concert and subsequently was given rabies shots at a nearby hospital.

    e. The capes used in bullfighting are red because the color enrages the animal and creates more active fights.

    f. The football team with the most NFL championships is the Pittsburgh Steelers, winners of six Super Bowls.

    g. A diet rich in carrots will improve a person's eyesight.

h. In the Open era, which began in 1968, the person with the most Wimbledon singles titles is Roger Federer with eight.

i. A penny dropped from the top of the Empire State Building will kill a person if it strikes him or her in the head.

j. Less than a month after Lynette "Squeaky" Fromme attempted to assassinate him, President Gerald Ford was shot by Sara Jane Moore in downtown San Francisco.

2. Conduct a "basic fact check" on the following sentences, examining them for spelling, numerical issues and other minor glitches.

a. The president of America lives and works at the White House, located at 1600 Pennsylvania Ave. NE, Washington, D.C.

b. Judge Neal Gorsuch was nominated to the Supreme Court of the United States to replace Justice Anthony Scalia, who died in 2015.

c. Marissa Tomei won the Emmy for Best Actress in 1992 for her role in "My Cousin Vinny."

d. Visitors to Manet's Gardens at Giverney can see the types of plants that inspired his paintings.

    e. Pittsburg Pirates infielder Daryl Ward hit for the cycle May 25, 2004, going 3 for 5 and driving in six runs.

3. Select a published news story, press release or other media report and fact-check it. Examine the piece for all of the "basic" issues, such as spelling, proper nouns, geographic elements and numerical concerns. In addition, assess the degree to which you can verify the broader issues with other sources. Finally, examine it for any vague terms or the use of hyperbole. Write a short essay that outlines what you found and how credible you find this piece of content to be as a result of your analysis.

GRAMMAR, STYLE AND LANGUAGE BASICS

REVIEW

1. According to the chapter, what are some important reasons grammar and style matter to you as a writer and your audience as readers?

2. What elements make up the "holy trinity" of a sentence?

3. What are the benefits of active-voice structure?

4. What is one way to find grammar or structural errors in your sentences, even if you aren't a grammar expert?

5. What is one way you can tell that your work has too many prepositional phrases?

6. What is an antecedent, and how does it relate to pronouns?

7. Name two important things to examine in the relationship between antecedents and pronouns.

8. What is a good way to avoid awkward construction or problems with antecedent-pronoun agreement caused by the lack of a gender-neutral pronoun?

WRITING EXERCISES

1. The sentences below contain at least one AP style error each. Locate the errors and make the appropriate corrections.

    a. I gave Reverend Jamie Stokes 1/3 of the money I had in my wallet after he gave a rousing sermon on the pulpit.

    b. Prof. Tim Gleason once lived at Four S. ash Boulevard in Akron, OH.

    c. After Senator John Kerry served in the Vietnam war, he received 3 purple hearts, 1 bronze star and 1 silver star.

    d. In the 1980's, Charles lived on S. Third St. in a 2 bedroom house.

    e. At 9PM, I met Jim at the movies to see Deadpool, starring Mr. Ryan Reynolds.

    f. When I turned sixteen, my Dad bought me a membership to the American Automobile Association so I never had to worry about my car breaking down.

    g. Jim attended Westminster college because he could get a 2 room suite in the dorms and a one thousand dollar scholarship.

    h. Even when he got four Fs on his report card, Barry's bad grades did not seem to phase him.

    i. When he heard the devastating news, the Governor declared that the flag at the capital should be lowered to half-mast.

    j. After he received her BA in Journalism, Tracy went to N.Y. and worked as a reporter for Newsweek Magazine.

    k. Jones lost the election for Senator in Wis. to Smith by a ratio of two to one.

    l. During WW 2, Sargent Bill Jones would always run towards danger to help people.

    m. When Zoe was three-years-old, we put her in a day care group for the Summer.

    n. When he drives on I-94, he usually exceeds 70 miles per hour.

o. Kaitlyn gave birth on August 17 to a healthy six pound, four ounce baby girl.

p. Nicky opened his gift on Christmas eve and discovered that he got a copy of Star Wars on DVD.

q. The fight between professor John Jones and chancellor Jayne Caufield was a year-long battle over a matter of five dollars.

r. Before I picked up Father Billy Watkins at Saint Paul's church, I asked the rental company for an up-grade because I was driving a Priest.

s. He joined the navy and began service in the seventh fleet right away.

t. The band played Satisfaction, which was a number one hit for the Rolling Stones back in the 60's.

2. Select the word that best completes each sentence.

   a. Clare and (she/her) went to the movies last weekend.
   b. I gave Roger and (he/him) a chance to come with us.
   c. I can't believe neither of (they/them) wanted to go.
   d. The class will take (its/their) final exam on Wednesday.
   e. The Cleveland Cavaliers will play (its/their) final game on Friday.
   f. Each member of the Cavaliers will practice (his/their) free throws before the game.
   g. The cat lost (its/it's) favorite toy under the couch.
   h. The ball wasn't thrown to (he/him) or (I/me), which is good because neither (he/him) nor (I/me) would have caught it.

3. Select the word that properly completes the sentence.

   a. (Among/Between) the six people in your house, who is the oldest?
   b. Jim told me he (definitely/defiantly) supported the president, backing every choice the leader made.
   c. As much as Chaz loved to win, he hated to (lose/loose) even more.
   d. After her car accident, Jillian was (racked/wracked) with pain every day.
   e. After a skunk sprayed him, Spot just (reeked/wreaked) for days.
   f. I tried to (brake/break) him of that habit, but Victor just would not stop smoking.
   g. I took my rod and (real/reel) down to the pond in hope of catching some fish.

    h.   After she lost her bid for Congress, Kayla's victory party essentially was (moot/mute).

    i.   He kept his father's old (plane/plain) in the (hangar/hanger) out back.

    j.   The (envelop/envelope) was unopened, but we all wanted to see what was inside.

    k.   When the Rev. Carlton Smith approached the (altar/alter), he (evoked/invoked) God to help lead his flock.

    l.   When Susie got to the baseball game, she found her seat in the middle of the (aisle/isle).

    m. Lilly's favorite comedy (troop/troupe) was performing at a theater on Smith Street.

    n.   The mayor (cited/sighted/sited) his favorite law during the debate.

    o.   Andrea seemed to have a (flair/flare) for the dramatic.

4.   Label each sentence as being written in active or passive voice:

    a.   Carl washed his best friend's car.

    b.   He was asked to clean it.

    c.   The car was dirty for quite some time.

    d.   Who lets a car get that filthy?

    e.   The pie was baked for the state fair.

    f.   The contest is judged each year by last year's winners.

    g.   Susie is going to win again this year for sure.

    h.   The mayor heard threats from several citizens this week.

    i.   I was told to throw the fish back in the lake.

    j.   Has anyone considered a change to the law?

    k.   The law was written almost 50 years ago.

    l.   It was created by some pretty bad legislators.

BASIC WRITING

REVIEW

1. What are the Killer "Be's" of good writing?

2. How should you order information in your story if you are using the inverted-pyramid format?

3. List the 5W's and 1H.

4. How does the chapter suggest that you should build a sentence?

5. How long should a lead be in a standard inverted-pyramid piece of writing?

6. Define and differentiate between a name-recognition lead and an interesting-action lead.

7. When writing an event lead, what should your lead include, and what should it not include?

8. What is the purpose of a second-day lead?

9. List the four types of problematic leads listed in the chapter.

10. According to the book, how long should most of your paragraphs be in a standard inverted-pyramid story?

WRITING EXERCISES

1. Read the following sentences and boil each of them down to a simple noun-verb-object structure (who did what to whom/what). Feel free to use words you don't find in the sentence, particularly if you want to use a stronger verb or a more concrete noun.

   - By a 4–1 vote, the Clarmont School Board decided Tuesday not to renew the contract of the high school's principal, Fred Hermann, after he was accused of financial misconduct over the past year.

   - The Chi Gamma Gamma sorority lost a member of its chapter to suicide last year and thus voted this week to perform a fundraiser to start an annual scholarship in that student's name.

   - Clete Rhome, the creator of a multimillion dollar time-management app, said he will likely consider several new ventures but is most interested in a run for president.

   - The Milsmith Owls scored two defensive touchdowns, rushed for three more and scored on a final-play two-point conversion to defeat the rival Oxbow Foxes, 43–42, on Friday.

   - The Campus Herald, the student newspaper at North Central College, is being accused of libel in a court filing by a professor, who was falsely accused in the paper of taking money for grades.

   - When the lottery numbers of 5, 12, 18, 42, 44 and 56 were announced in this month's Big Winner drawing, Mickey Meister, a local homeless man, found himself $485 million richer.

2. **EVENT-LEAD PRACTICE**

Use each of these chunks of text to create a solid event lead that has a sharp focus and avoids drawing attention to the event itself:

   a. Facebook founder and CEO Mark Zuckerberg gave a speech to the annual Facebook developers conference today. He laid out his vision for the next 10 years of social media and explained that he saw video as vital. Zuckerberg said that video will connect all people, not just the wealthiest people, to all the opportunities of the internet. He compared the importance of video in 10 years in terms of content sharing and connectivity to the way mobile communication became essential over these previous 10 years. The company's goal with video is to give everyone everywhere the ability to share anything they want with anyone else.

   b. The Board of Trustees at Northwest Central State College met Tuesday to discuss several key issues. The main issue on the table was the cost of education and how it affects the quality of education. With diminishing state funds, the school was losing many faculty members who were in key areas of research and teaching. The school also had to eliminate several classes because it lacked the resources to teach them. The board agreed to raise tuition this year by 3 percent to improve course offerings and raise it another 3 percent next year to offer pay increases to faculty. The board passed this plan by a 9–0 vote.

c. Jacoby Everson, the chancellor of Eastern State University, held a press conference today to announce some changes to the institution. He said he remembered being a new faculty member on campus almost 40 years ago, and he marveled at how much the university has grown in that time. He mentioned that his past 20 years, when he has served as chancellor, have been among the happiest of his life. However, he wanted to make a change in life, so at the end of this year, he will be retiring.

d. Bethany Swarf, a two-time gold-medal-winning gymnast for the United States, came to Big State University on Tuesday and gave a speech. She said becoming an Olympic gymnast involved a lot of work and a lot of pain. She has broken many bones, sprained every joint in her arms and legs multiple times and sustained at least six concussions. As a result, she met with doctors, who she often felt did not help her as much as they should have but rather tried to "patch me up and get me back in there before I was healthy." She said this forced her to retire from the sport at the age of 21, which is when she decided to go public about these issues. Her decision, she said, led to many other young women speaking out and a total reversal of medical practices in the sport. She said she knows she will never be able to leave her wheelchair, a result of a severed spine from an undiagnosed back fracture, but she said she felt good that other gymnasts might not face such issues.

3. LEAD-REWRITING PRACTICE

Below are several problematic leads. Rewrite them to eliminate the specific problem associated with each lead and to improve their overall readability:

- You should attend the 4 p.m. pep rally Friday outside Memorial Stadium for our Eastern High School team as they prepare for the annual rivalry game against Western High School.

- Have you ever wondered what it would be like to find buried treasure? Archeology professor Harold Smith figures everyone has at one point, which is why he converted his summer class into a study-abroad opportunity to search for missing valuables at a former pirate stronghold along the Barbary Coast.

- Everybody has been hungry at one point in class and been without food. This is why Central College student Albert Todello created his "Campus Cravings" app, which connects students who need a snack with his delivery service that will bring granola bars, popcorn or a protein shake right into the classroom.

- Imagine living a life without your parents and wondering how or why they abandoned you at an orphanage. Bill Smith, this year's valedictorian, said it was his life growing up in the Child Protective Services system that inspired him to become both a social worker and a good parent.

4. BRIEF-WRITING PRACTICE

Use the information below to create a four-paragraph, inverted-pyramid brief. Each paragraph should be one sentence long and should attribute the information to your source. The first sentence is your lead, and the remaining three paragraphs should be organized so that information is presented in descending order of importance.

Source: Lt. Sam Sires, Beacontown Fire Department

INFORMATION: The Beacontown Fire Department responded to a call around 2 a.m. Wednesday of a potential fire in the area of Broadway and Fifth Avenue. Chief's Car 6, Pumper Truck 5, Engine Company 8 and other support vehicles responded as a result. Firefighters arrived at 1002 N. Fifth Ave. to find the one-story, three-bedroom home fully enveloped in flames. The homeowners, Wendy Walther and Zeke Walther, were outside of the home, as was their daughter, Fiona. No one was left inside. Nobody was injured.

Firefighters deployed several hose lines and fought the blaze for five hours until getting full control of the situation. Two fire marshals eventually were able to enter the remains of the home to determine the cause of the blaze. They stated that the fire began when a space heater tipped over in the living room and ignited a couch. The fire then spread along the room's ceiling, which consisted mostly of very old wood.

The home is considered a total loss, and the loss is estimated to be $300,000 in damages.

5. BRIEF-WRITING PRACTICE

Use the information below to create a four-paragraph, inverted-pyramid brief. Each paragraph should be one sentence long and should attribute the information to your source. The first sentence is your lead and the remaining three paragraphs should be organized so that information is presented in descending order of importance.

Source: Melanie Danbury, head of the University of Springfield's student health center

INFORMATION: Last week, we began receiving reports that several students in the residence halls were becoming ill. Around that time, we also had seen an increase in walk-in traffic at the health center. The students in the residence halls and those students who came to our offices complained of stomach cramps, diarrhea and vomiting. Some students had also become massively dehydrated as a result of these symptoms. Those students were taken to University Hospital for treatment.

We collected several forms of samples from these individuals and found a common thread in their illness. These students were suffering from Escherichia bacterial poisoning, more commonly known as E. coli poisoning. As we worked our way through the treatment of these students, we began to experience a continuing stream of students with similar symptoms entering the health center. They, too, were tested for and found to have E. coli poisoning.

After conducting interviews with as many of the patients as possible, we were able to determine that all of the individuals had been eating frequently at Bob's Café, the food-service eatery within the Nelson Residence Hall Complex. In addition, they all noted consuming some form of meat from the café. We immediately reached out to the university's food staff and closed Bob's Café until further notice as we conducted an investigation of this potential contagion.

Today, we are releasing the results of our report. It appears that a refrigeration unit at Bob's Café had broken down, leaving the meat within that unit at an unsafe temperature. It is our finding that E. coli bacteria spread throughout the meat in that unit and has led to this outbreak of illness.

Students who have eaten at Bob's Café, especially those with weakened immune systems and those who ate meat frequently over the past week, should immediately come to the health center for examination. If you note the presence of any of these symptoms, regardless of where you have been eating, contact the health center immediately. To prevent the spread of this illness, students should wash their hands frequently as well as wash any utensils and food-serving items. We have also set up a page on the university's website to answer any additional questions you may have.

INTERVIEWING

REVIEW

1. Before you interview a subject, you need to conduct research on that person. Name several places the chapter states you could find background information on your subject.

2. What are the pros and cons of an email interview? When should you use them, and when should you avoid them?

3. When you contact someone to set up an interview, what should you tell this person?

4. What is a loaded question, and why is it bad?

5. What is the primary difference between an open-ended question and a closed-ended question?

6. According to the book, about how many prepared questions should you have for a standard news interview?

7. What is the best way to make sure you can record your interview on audio or video equipment?

8. What are two ways you can encourage your source to elaborate on a topic without asking another question?

9. What are two good questions to ask a source once you are done with your main set of questions?

WRITING EXERCISES

1. Prepare to interview someone important at your school. This could be the head of the school, a star athlete or anyone you think would have a compelling story. Conduct research on this person, and write up a page or so of information on that person you think might be valuable in helping you craft several questions that would make for a good interview.

2. On the basis of the research you conducted, write three or four closed-ended questions and three or four open-ended questions. Make sure you select the type of question properly to best elicit the type of response you want. For example, if you asked the mayor about allegations that he failed to pay his taxes, you would probably want a hard confirmation or denial up front, so a closed-ended question might be best. On the other hand, if you interview an athlete about a miraculous final play in a championship game, you would likely want an open-ended question so the source could elaborate.

3. Below is a list of poorly worded questions. Rewrite them to fix the problems associated with them (or come up with a better overall question), and then explain why your version of the question is better than the initial question.

    - "Coach, how many more bad decisions does quarterback Brett Belter have to make until you bench him?"

    - "Senator, talk about the rationale behind your bill that would ban the use of nut-based products on airplanes after one of your grandchildren went into anaphylactic shock during a flight."

    - "Mr. Jones, I know your wife just died in a car accident. How do you feel about that?"

    - "President Trump, did you ever think you would become president of the United States?"

    - "After three losses in a row, Coach, don't you think the fans have a right to demand you be fired?"

    - "When you first met your husband, were you alone at the diner or were you just by yourself?"

    - "Mr. Mayor, you had concerns about the voting process, which some people said was rigged, but do you feel that's not true now only because you won?"

    - "When were you born on your birthday?"

    - "How many of your comeback wins came when the other team was ahead?"

    - "I know your company was purchased recently by a group out of Japan, China or Canada, so which one was it?"

4. Watch a news interview that a broadcast journalist conducted live on air. It could be during a Sunday morning talk show or a longer clip on YouTube. Analyze the purpose of the interview and the value of the person being interviewed in relation to the topic. Do you think the interview worked well overall? Why or why not? How did the interviewer use questions and statements to gather information? Choose one or two questions that you think were particularly good, and explain why you thought they worked. Choose one or two questions that you think were particularly problematic, and explain how you would have reworked the questions to improve them.

INTERVIEWING EXERCISE

Select a person of interest to you, and work your way through the interview process listed in the chapter with him or her. Start by asking for an interview via email or telephone. Include your interview's purpose, your deadline and how much time you will need for the interview. Find a place to interview the person in a face-to-face setting. Prepare for the interview by researching the person and crafting about four or five good questions on the basis of your research. Conduct the interview and take good notes. If possible, record the interview as well so you can compare your notes with what the person actually said.

WRITING ON THE WEB

REVIEW

1. What is one of the biggest challenges associated with writing on the web, and why is it a challenge?

2. What is "shovelware," and why is it bad?

3. Name three things you can do that will make your content more valuable on the web.

4. What is a blog?

5. What are some of the benefits to blogging for news? For promotional areas like PR, advertising and marketing?

6. What does the chapter mean when it states that you need to "establish a tone" on your blog?

7. How can you use linking to augment your blog and serve your audience?

WRITING EXERCISES

1. Select a website that you frequently use and analyze it on the basis of the key elements noted at the beginning of the chapter. Does it avoid "shovelware" and produce original content not available on a traditional media platform or any other digital platform? Does it use multiple elements, such as audio, video, links, graphics, photos and text, to tell stories, or does it rely primarily on one element? Does it contain short, easy-to-use pieces, or does it fail to contain its content to user-friendly pieces? How frequently does it update its content, and is this enough for the type of website it is (news, promotional etc.) and the expectations you have as a reader? Write a short essay on your experience on the site and your answers to these questions.

2. Select a news blog and determine how well it takes advantage of the benefits outlined in the chapter. Does it provide additional content, or does it rely on shovelware? Does it provide content in niche areas, or does it cover traditional beat areas with extra material? How often is the blog updated, and what kinds of material are on the blog? Given what you know about the audience for this blog, does it serve its readers well? Write a short essay on your findings.

3. Select a promotional blog that is owned and operated by a public relations agency, an advertising firm or a corporation of some kind. How does this blog reach its audience through the provision of content? Does it humanize the organization and provide the readers with a sense of connectivity to the people who work there? Does it reinforce the focus and vision of the organization in a clear and coherent fashion? Does it showcase its position as an authority on the topics covered on the blog? How often is it updated, and what kinds of material are on the blog? Given what you know about the audience for this blog, does it serve its readers well? Write a short essay on your findings.

4. Select a topic of interest to your campus and develop a story web for it. Develop no fewer than four key factors that play directly into the core of the topic. Create several key pieces that can extend from each of those key factors, as well as ways in which you would present those pieces (text, audio, video, graphics etc.). Finally, draw pathways between clearly congruent topics you could see readers following after reading each piece. Then, write a short essay on your topic, your approach to it and why you built the elements and pathways the way you did.

5. Review a series of blogs on an area of interest to you. Assess them with regard to how well they focus on audience interests, establish a tone, provide timely information and offer quick reads. Explain in a short essay what drew you to these blogs. What makes them worth reading? How well do they serve you and other audience members with similar interests? What are some ways in which you feel the content could be improved on the basis of your needs and the topics discussed in this chapter?

6. Either develop a blog that covers a niche topic of interest that matters to you or join the staff of a blog that fits these parameters. On the basis of the type of blog you join (news or promotional), sketch out several posts that you think would best meet the needs of the readers and fulfill some of the basic elements outlined under each of these types of blogs listed in the chapter. Develop an approach to deliver content to readers and drive traffic to your posts. Then maintain an active schedule of posting for that blog over the course of a week. Make sure to respond to any comments you receive and correct any errors of which you become aware.

SOCIAL MEDIA

REVIEW

1. Define social media. What are some of the key characteristics associated with it?

2. What does the term "viral" mean, and how can the viral nature of social media be both good and bad for users?

3. A tweet should have what at its core?

4. What are some benefits of placing content on social networking sites like Facebook and LinkedIn?

5. According to the chapter, what are some steps you can take to avoid creating a viral failure on a social media platform?

6. The experts at IMPACT list a few tips that can help you build and maintain a social media audience. Name them.

7. What is the 70/20/10 rule, and how does it work?

WRITING EXERCISES

1. Go through the list of sources you follow on one of your social media platforms and categorize them on the basis of who they are (media outlets, celebrities, family members etc.). What does each source category you created provide to you in terms of value? Apply the FOCII elements to the sources and the content they provide. Which elements apply to which groups? What do you think this says about your media consumption habits on this platform?

2. On the basis of the type of content you produce on a social media platform, sketch out whom you believe to be your typical follower. Then, go through your list of followers and analyze them according to those presuppositions. How accurate was your sketch, and what does it say about how well you know your audience on this platform?

3. Select the Twitter feed of a media source you follow and review about a week's worth of posts to see if this source follows the 70/20/10 rule. If it doesn't, what is the approximate balance among these three areas, and to what degree do you see that being problematic? If the source follows this rule, what kinds of original content does it post, what kinds of content does it share from other sources and what types of promotional content does it post? Write a short piece on this topic.

4. Select five tweets from a professional media source or a media professional in your area that are at least 240 characters. Edit these tweets for clarity, structure and value, and see if you can get them to be short enough to work under the old 140-character limit.

5. Rewrite the following tweets to tighten the writing, improve the structure and sharpen the focus:

   - Immigration officials have arrested a Montana-based man who was a "local doctor" who immigrated from Estonia when he was a child and has a green card. Officers say he committed two minor property crimes more than 25 years ago, when he was 17 and that makes him trouble.

   - The federal government shutdown has led to furloughs of just over half of the governmental employees in the country, shutting down what it deems "non-essential resources," including some popular monuments and parks popular with tourists—like the Statue of Liberty.

   - City workers in Philadelphia took to the streets Sunday to apply greasy Crisco to light poles and other tall street-side structures to prevent Philadelphia Eagles fans from climbing them after the NFC championship game. They call themselves the Crisco Cops.

   - Each year, Mixton Soup Company (@mixsoupco) hosts annual "Soup Up Your Health" fitness walk. Rain is in the forecast for Wednesday, so look for the "Soup Up Your Health" race to move elsewhere. The Oboye North High School indoor track will serve as walking site if rain hits.

   - Speaker @Iknowstuff: The difficult and tricky thing about online learning is it's easy to do it alone, but that's not how we do our best. There's a clear benefit to learning from each other's perceptions/questions. That's the value of social networks so we must involve them.

6. Select a media organization (newspaper, magazine, television station, PR firm, advertising corporation, marketing group etc.) and find four or five recent postings the group has made to its website. These could be news stories, press releases, blog posts or any other form of content that is likely useful, valuable and engaging for its readership. Then, craft a tweet of no more than 240 characters to promote each of these pieces. Remember to construct a solid noun-verb-object core and remain focused on one key point in your tweet.

7. Find an example of a social media disaster that went viral. (As an example, the book includes the #AskJamies campaign and the #WhyIStayed incident from DiGiorno Pizza as examples.) Locate the source of the disaster (bad tweet, ugly photo, horrible video post), and explain what went wrong and where the backlash came from. Then, explain what the person or company responsible for the original disaster did or said in response to the backlash. How could this have been avoided, and how well did the sender do at addressing the disaster? What lessons do you think could be learned from the situation?

LAW AND ETHICS

REVIEW

1. What are the freedoms delineated in the First Amendment to the Constitution?

2. List and define the three types of limitations placed on free speech that are outlined in the chapter.

3. According to the book, what is the difference between "free" press or speech and "consequence-free" press or speech?

4. Define libel and list the things the chapter notes are required of a plaintiff to bring a legitimate libel suit.

5. What is the difference between actual and punitive damages in a libel suit?

6. List the defenses against libel outlined in the chapter. Which one do you find to be most effective and why?

7. What is copyright and why is it important for media professionals?

8. Compare and contrast fair use and creative commons. Explain how each of these items can help media professionals avoid copyright infringement.

9. What does the term "payola" mean, and how does it relate to media professionals in news and promotional fields?

10. List the four steps noted in the chapter that help you work through an ethical dilemma.

WRITING EXERCISES

1. Of the five ethical paradigms listed in the chapter, which one do you feel best fits your own approach to ethics? Explain why this one fits you best and how you use its tenets to deal with ethical situations in everyday life. Look at the remaining ethical philosophies and think about which one best fits someone with whom you have the greatest ethical divide. What is it about that person and his or her approach to ethics that rubs you the wrong way?

2. On the basis of the seven key elements necessary to win a libel suit, assess each of the following statements to determine if they meet the standard of libel. Write a few sentences for each one to justify your answer.

    - A student journalist issues a false and defamatory statement about another student on your campus but states that the information was only sent by Twitter and thus isn't subject to libel laws.

    - A sorority on campus issues a press release stating that its recruiting event will be "10 times better than whatever sad crap the losers at Zeta Zeta Zeta will do."

    - You publish a story about a professor on your campus who has a second job as "Muffy the Clown," performing at children's birthday parties. The professor is embarrassed that this information is now known and threatens to sue you.

    - A promising local band has a gig at the biggest event in the city. The music critic from the local paper writes a scathing review of the band for his weekly "Musical Notes" column. The band subsequently loses several other paying gigs and threatens to sue the writer and the paper for damages.

- While running for student body president against the sitting vice president, candidate Michael Jones issues a press release that states, "You definitely don't want to vote for my opponent because she has given herpes to almost everyone involved in student government." When pressed as to how he knows this, he refuses to present evidence related to this issue and says, "Hey, I didn't name her, but, y'know, anything's possible."

- The student newspaper analyzes records of grades handed out by professors at your university and finds that approximately 1 out of every 15 professors inflates grades. After the story is published, a professor of sociology calls the paper and threatens to sue for libel because of the story.

3. Below is a series of incidents in which the person involved files a lawsuit against you for libel. For each one, state whether you think someone suing you for libel would win. If you think you are safe, cite the specific defense outlined in the chapter that you think protects you.

   - Carl Smith is convicted of murder in a court of law. You later write a story about an appeal he has filed and you refer to him as "convicted killer Carl Smith."

   - In a story about a car crash, you quote a police officer who tells you that the driver of the Honda Civic, Jim Jacoby, was intoxicated when he caused the accident. After further investigation, it turns out the officer was wrong.

   - During a review of a local band, you write, "The Disco Points should be called 'The Disappoints' because that's all they did at Friday night's concert." The lead singer of the band has filed suit against you.

   - You overhear two professors on campus talking about a secretary in their office and how she probably steals money from the department. You send out a tweet that states "Secretary Wendy Waxington of the history department steals money." It turns out to be untrue, but you did delete the tweet after only 10 minutes, and you tweeted an apology.

   - You are writing a press release for your client, who just won a large settlement against an area company that was convicted of "discharging higher than acceptable levels of a chemical known to be harmful to humans" into an area stream. You write that your client "defeated Chemico and its president, Nate Schneller, who were responsible for spreading a deadly poison in area waterways."

   - After you get a failing grade in a journalism class, you post the following on a "Rate the Professor" website: "The only way to get through Journalism 222 with Dr. Charles Yoder is with money. If you can come up with the $500 he charges per A, you are fine. If not, you will never pass." You realize 20 minutes later that this wasn't a smart thing to do because it isn't true, so you delete it. However, screen shots of your post are now being shared on social media all over school.

4. Below is a series of incidents in which the person involved files a lawsuit against you for copyright infringement. For each one, state whether you think someone suing you would win or not. Give a rationale for your answer.

    •   You want to include photos of several types of vegetables on your press release about "Eat Healthy Week" at your school. You do an internet search and find several great photos from the same source, a studio photographer based in a nearby town. You just grab the photos off the web and use them. The photographer files suit against you for failing to obtain permission in advance or purchase the photos from his website.

    •   You visit a Creative Commons site to find photos of college-age students enjoying a party to promote your fraternity's annual "Dance the Night Away" event. You find a photo whose owner requires the image to be "passed along unchanged and in whole" but allows it to be used for all purposes, including commercial, if you credit the owner. You abide by all of these standards and use the image to promote the event. The image's owner contacts you and says that he has a strong dislike for fraternities and sororities and never would have allowed his image to be used by these groups. He files a suit against you.

    •   A famous alumna is returning to campus to launch her new movie and meet with current students. As the editor of the student newspaper, you decide to run a big spread on her, including photos of her when she was much younger. You contact her mother and ask for any images she shot and for permission to use them. The mother sends you several photos, including a few of the alumna in her "geeky awkward teen phase," with a note saying, "I shot these myself. Use whatever you want however you want." The alumna gets wind of this and files suit against you for violating copyright.

    •   A student from your school has been arrested on suspicion of robbing several area gas stations. The police are unable to provide you with a mugshot of this person, because the station's computer system is down. You find a selfie this person took posted to one of his social media accounts, so you crop it down to a mugshot and run it with your report in the student newspaper. The student sues you for "stealing my selfie."

5. Review the ethical code of an organization of media professionals in your chosen area or interest (Society of Professional Journalists, National Press Photographers Association, Public Relations Society of America, American Advertising Federation etc.). What are some topics the code covers and some of the values the group espouses? How important are these issues to you personally? Do you see potential conflict between your values and those of this organization?

6. If you chose a code in a promotional field for exercise 5, choose a code from a news organization, or vice versa. Compare and contrast the code from the organization to which you relate with this code. What are the similarities and differences? Are there any aspects of these codes that you find to be incompatible? What are they, and why do you feel that way?

7. Review the following ethical dilemmas and apply your ethical paradigm. How would you use your paradigm and the suggestions from your ethical code to guide your actions?

- You are a local reporter working on a "Chaos of Christmas Shopping" story. A local merchant is selling a "must-have toy" that parents are lining up around the block to get each time a shipment arrives. Even your own family members are obsessed with getting one of these toys. The merchant has agreed to your request to cover the chaos when he gets a new shipment, and he has let you into the store before it opens for the day. Just before he lets everyone else know about the shipment, he offers you the chance to buy one or two. Do you buy the toy?

- Envision the same scenario above, but instead of being a reporter, you are a public relations practitioner for the city's Local Merchants Association, and you are there to gather content to promote the store and the association. Do you buy the toy?

- You are working on a story about a bank robbery, and the police are not releasing the name of the man who was arrested on suspicion of robbing the bank. You receive a phone call from your neighbor, with whom you have had several unpleasant encounters, mostly due to his son's playing music too loudly or leaving garbage on your lawn.

  He says he knows you work at the local TV station and your colleagues are probably working on the bank robbery story. "Look," he says. "I know we have a lot of disagreements, but I'm *begging* you not to put my son's name on TV as the robber. He's a good kid who made a dumb mistake. He even called me from jail to ask me to ask you for forgiveness and mercy." Given that this is your only source of information for the name, do you run the name of the son as the robber?

- Consider the same scenario as above, but imagine the person calling you for help were your best friend or a close family member? Would you run the name then?

- You are a public relations practitioner who is assigned to cover the state high school track championship for the State Track Association's newsletter and website. The main story everyone wants to know about involves a student from the local high school who lost his brother to cancer one day before the tournament. In a major upset, the student wins the 100-meter dash, setting a state record. In celebration, he runs to the stands, grabs a framed photo of his brother and does a victory lap, holding the photo aloft.

  Unfortunately for you, traffic was horrible, and you missed the whole thing. The student knows you and offers to take another lap with the photo so you can shoot the photo of him. Because no other media outlet covered the event, no one will ever know that you weren't there on time, and he promises not to tell anyone. What do you do?

- A senator from your state is likely to face a fierce reelection campaign this year, as a formidable challenger from an opposition party has emerged. The senator has spent the past two years working on various projects with underprivileged students throughout the state and will likely make this a big part of his campaign.

The senator contacts your news outlet and asks if you would be interested in going on a two-week junket throughout the state, during which he will visit these areas and check in on all of his ongoing projects. The campaign will pay all of your expenses, such as hotel and food costs, and you will have complete access to the senator and anyone else involved with those projects. Your boss has always left decisions like this up to the individual reporter. What would you do?

- You are responsible for a senate campaign, including everything from press contacts to public events to advertising. An anonymous source drops off a packet of material outside your home that contains damaging information about your opponent's wife. It seems the wife had several affairs while married to the candidate and had been known to abuse prescription pain medication. No laws were broken and no arrests were ever made, but you have emails between the wife and several people that support these claims. This is a tight race, and any advantage you get could make the difference. Do you release this information to the press? Do you have your candidate make any kind of public statement using this information? Do you create an advertising campaign that uses this information as its core?

REPORTING: THE BASICS AND BEYOND

REVIEW

1. List and explain the major types of events the chapter notes you might see in a reporting career.

2. What does it mean to "shell a story," what does a "shell" include and how does "shelling a story" benefit you as a reporter?

3. What does it mean to "look outside the lines" at an event?

4. What is beat reporting and how does it work? Give an example of a thematic beat you would expect a local news outlet to cover frequently.

5. What is a news peg, and what question does it answer about a feature story?

6. When you report for a profile, what are three things you should look for in terms of observation?

7. List three things that will make for a good localization story.

8. List three things that make for a bad localization story.

9. What is an obituary?

WRITING EXERCISES

1. Find coverage of a local speech or meeting in a news outlet you trust. Examine the story to ascertain what the key points of the speech or meeting were. How well did the reporter do at conveying information that matches up with the FOCII elements outlined in the book? How clear was the reporter in explaining why the main points of the story mattered to the audience members who were reading it? What could have been done better?

2. Look for a notice of a speech, meeting or news conference that is happening near you, and prepare for it like you would if you had to write a story for a local publication. What information did you need to gather in advance of the event? Use some of that information to create a "shell" of a story. Then, attend the event and see what happens. Write a solid lead and some additional content on the basis of what you witnessed and what you believe to be the key elements of the event. Look for coverage on this event in local media outlets the next day and compare and contrast your coverage to their work as part of an essay to accompany the short story you wrote.

3. Select a beat area that interests you and spend at least two weeks exploring the area. Make a list of at least three people who have some stake in that beat who might have

interesting story ideas for you. Search through at least one set of documents on your beat for potential story ideas. Then, come up with three potential story ideas you think would be valuable, useful and interesting to a local audience on the basis of what you have found on your beat.

4. Find a reporter who covers a beat that interests you. This could be someone who covers high school football, the police department or science and technology issues. Read at least five recent stories or blog posts this individual has published, and then contact the beat reporter for a potential interview. Find out as much as you can about how beat reporting works, including the great stuff and the not-so-great stuff.

5. Unplug from all of your electronic devices for no less than four hours with the intention of finding potential feature stories. Listen to other people's conversations at the school cafeteria or in line at the coffee shop. Look at various historical markers on your campus, and read any postings you find on kiosks or bulletin boards. Sit on a bench and observe people as they move all around you as you seek trends in clothing, transportation or anything else. Find at least three story ideas you think would be good for news features. For each, write up a short paragraph as to what you think the story is, why it would matter to your audience and who might make for good sources.

6. Read at least three long-form personality profiles on people who interest you. They can be published in magazines, in the newspaper or on the web. How well did the writers do at providing you with a complete and complex understanding of this person? Who was interviewed, and what insights did they provide? How much observation was done, and can you see the person in your mind's eye? Write up a short analysis of what you found and the ways in which you think this could have been done better or differently.

7. Review national news sources for stories that could have a local impact. Select a story topic you feel would make for a good localization, and write up a short paragraph as to why you think this topic would matter to people in your area. Then, conduct some research to find at least three human sources you think would be helpful to you if you were to write your localization, and explain why you think so. Write all of this up in a short paper.

8. Read a local or national publication's obituary page. Compare the standard "paid obituaries" with the "news obituaries" written about noteworthy people. What features are the same in these forms of obituary, and what elements are different?

WRITING FOR TRADITIONAL PRINT NEWS PRODUCTS

REVIEW

1. Explain the concept of objectivity and why it matters to news writers.

2. List and define the three types of quotes outlined in this chapter.

3. What are the positive and negative aspects associated with altering direct quotes?

4. What is an attribution, how does it work and what is the preferred verb of attribution?

5. According to the chapter, what is the most grammatically correct structure for an attribution?

6. Where does a bridge occur in an expanded inverted-pyramid story, and what are some examples of things that make for good bridges?

7. What does the book suggest would make for a good closing paragraph?

WRITING EXERCISES

1. Review the following statements to determine if you think you would need to attribute the information to a source. Remember, you do not need to attribute material if the content is a statement of fact or something clearly observable. Opinions, however, require attribution.

   a. Author Betty Smith wrote the book "A Tree Grows in Brooklyn."
   b. The school bus crashed into a ditch, but luckily, only one student died.
   c. Point Barrow, Alaska, is the northernmost point in all U.S. territory.
   d. The Green Bay Packers beat the Dallas Cowboys 21–17 on Dec. 31, 1967.
   e. People who live in Alabama don't know how to handle cold weather.
   f. By a 5–4 vote, the Supreme Court made a horrible ruling in Miller v. California.
   g. If you have the flu or flu-like symptoms, you should stay at home for at least 24 hours after your fever is gone.
   h. The Cleveland Browns amassed a record of 0–16 in 2017, tying them for the worst single-season record in National Football League history.
   i. The Cleveland Browns are the worst team in National Football League history.

2. Below is the transcript of a speech delivered by Vice President Mike Pence to Young America's Foundation on Aug. 4, 2017. Select three direct quotes that you think have value, and write them up in a properly attributed structure. Then, write a one-sentence paragraph of paraphrase for each quote. Paraphrase should identify the speaker, set up the quote with complementary (but not repetitive) information and seamlessly transition into the direct quote. Then, write a short reflection essay that explains why you picked these quotes and why you think they work well with the paragraphs of paraphrase you composed.

Hyatt Regency Capitol Hill
Washington, D.C.
7:00 P.M. EDT

THE VICE PRESIDENT: Thank you for that wonderful, warm welcome. And thank you to my friend Frank Donatelli for that overly generous introduction.

   Frank knows me well enough to know the introduction I prefer is just a little bit shorter. I'm a Christian, a conservative, and a Republican—in that order. (Applause.)

   And I's a great honor to be here tonight to address the rising generation of conservative leaders, the men and women of Young America's Foundation, here at the 39th National Conservative Student Conference. Give yourselves a round of applause. You're going to be making a difference in America for a long time. (Applause.)

So welcome back to Washington, D.C. Before I get started, I bring greetings this evening from a friend of mine, a man who's fighting every day for common-sense, conservative values—from the very heart of the White House in the Oval Office, I bring greetings from the 45th President of the United States of America—President Donald Trump. (Applause.)

Thanks to the support of so many young conservatives like all of you here today all across this country, last November President Trump won a historic victory. More counties than any President since Ronald Reagan—30 of 50 states, states no Republican had carried in a generation. The truth is with your support, President Donald Trump turned the blue wall red. (Applause.)

And I came here tonight just to pay a debt of gratitude to all of you who helped elect a President who is fighting every day, fighting every day for the values and the ideals that unite us, and fighting every day to keep the promises that he made to the American people.

And for my part, it's a privilege to be back at the Young America's Foundation. I've worked hand-in-hand with YAF going back more than 15 years—not from when that picture was taken. (Laughter.) But from when I first arrived in Congress in 2001. In 2005, my family had the great privilege to visit the Reagan Ranch, where YAF has wonderfully preserved the wisdom and legacy of my second favorite President of the United States, President Ronald Reagan. (Applause.)

I have to tell you as I ran into Ron and Frank backstage, thinking of all the years that we've stood together and all the encouragement they've been to me as a conservative, I just can't tell you how genuinely humbling it is for me to think that I'm standing before you today because of their encouragement, and support and because of folks like you all over this country, and because of the confidence and generosity of our new President that I stand before you today as the 48th Vice President of the United States of America. So on behalf of my family, thank you for the opportunity to serve. (Applause.)

It's remarkable to think about the Young America's Foundation's history and contributions not just to my small life but to the conservative movement itself and to this entire country.

Since its founding in 1960, YAF has been a bulwark of American greatness. You fight for the truths of the Declaration of Independence and the Constitution. You fight for those timeless principles of "individual freedom, a strong national defense, free enterprise, and traditional moral values". And let there be no doubt because of the work of all of you all across this country, conservative values are winning on campuses and winning the hearts and minds of America one student at a time. (Applause.)

Today, YAF has more than 300 chapters that are active on over 2,000 campuses all across the United States, reaching a stunning 400,000 students every year.

You run so many noteworthy projects and programs, but I'd especially like to thank you particularly for your heroic work promoting and standing for freedom of expression and the free exchange of ideas on the campuses across this country. (Applause.)

As I said in an address I gave at the University of Notre Dame just a few months ago, we live in a time when free speech and civility are waning on campuses across America, but YAF is committed to change that. And you're making a great difference.

You've speaking out against speech codes, safe spaces, political correctness. You fight to defend conservative speakers and students who want nothing more than to exercise their First Amendment right to the freedom of speech.

And so tonight, I just want to say thank you. Thank you to the young men and women of Young America's Foundation for your strong stand for our freedoms, and thank you for all that you do, day-in and day-out to bring the conservative message to the public square. (Applause.)

And I can promise you as you labor, I see it every day, the Young America's Foundation finally has a friend back in the Oval Office in the White House. (Applause.)

President Donald Trump has been fighting every day for the conservative vision, the conservative values that you and I hold dear.

President Trump has given voice I believe to the aspirations and frustrations of the American people like no leader since President Ronald Reagan.

And our President has gone right to work putting men and women into a Cabinet and into this administration that have been advancing that agenda with consistency and with courage.

I got to tell you I think President Donald Trump has assembled the strongest conservative Cabinet in my lifetime—bar none. (Applause.) Think about it. How about Ambassador Nikki Haley to the United Nations? (Applause.) How about Dr. Ben Carson at Housing and Urban Development? (Applause.) In fact, I know you're going to hear from Dr. Carson tonight, and he's just an incredible member of this Cabinet—right along with others like Secretary of Defense Jim "Mad Dog" Mattis. (Applause.)

You go around that table and people like Betsy DeVos and others, truly it speaks volumes about this President's commitment to surrounding himself with extraordinary men and women as a part of this administration's team, and I couldn't be more proud to be a small part of it.

So as I stand before you today, I'm deeply humbled to be able to report to you that not just in assembling this team, but since day one of this administration, this President has been putting conservative principles into practice to strengthen America at home and abroad so that your generation can live in a country that is prosperous, safe, and free and is built on the highest ideals of the American experience. (Applause.)

Just look at what our President has done to get the American economy moving again already. President Trump I'm pleased to report has actually signed more laws cutting through federal red tape than any President in American history. (Applause.) This President has been unleashing American energy after years of frustration by a liberal administration like when he authorized the construction of the Keystone and Dakota pipelines. (Applause.) And begun to roll back the Clean Power Plan. The truth is under President Donald Trump, the war on coal is over. (Applause.)

And this President has been putting America first, like when he announced that the United States of America officially today notified the United Nations that we are withdrawing from the Paris climate accord. (Applause.)

In a word, President Trump been keeping his promise to make America prosperous again. Just this morning, the news came in—did you hear about it? Over 1 million new jobs have been created across this country by businesses large and small since President Donald Trump took office. More Americans working than ever before, and unemployment hasn't been this low in 16 years. And as the President tweeted this morning, we "have only just begun"! (Applause.)

But as important as our prosperity is, this President knows that security is the foundation of our prosperity. And serving with him every day, I can assure you, President Trump has no higher priority than the safety and security of the American people.

Our President has travelled across the wider world, reaffirming our historic alliances, challenging all who cherish freedom to step up and confront the forces that threaten our way of life. President Trump I'm pleased to report—once again, we have a President who stands without apology on the world stage as leader of the free world. (Applause.)

And I have to tell you more personal to me, as the proud father of a United States Marine, I couldn't be more grateful to serve as Vice President to a President who cares so deeply about the men and women of the Armed Forces of the United States, their families, and our veterans. (Applause.)

The United States of America simply has the finest armed forces in the history of the world. The men and women who wear the uniform of this country are the best of your generation, and I'm inspired whenever I'm among them. Today, at Dover Air Force Base two heroes of this generation came home. Sergeant Jonathon Hunter and Specialist Christopher Harris of the 82nd Airborne. These two heroes fell defending our freedom in Afghanistan this week. We honor their service and their sacrifice. Their names will be enshrined in the hearts of a grateful nation, and their families and their loved ones will remain our prayers. For no greater love has a man than this, that he should lay down his life for his friends. These two men were heroes. We honor them tonight by standing with all those who at this very hour stand a far distant post on the ramparts of freedom. God bless them all. (Applause.)

And we honor them through our tributes, but we also honor them through our actions. And I'll make you a promise: President Donald Trump is going to be the best friend the Armed Forces of the United States will have ever had in the White House. (Applause.)

You think about it, our President has already signed the largest increase in military spending in nearly 10 years. And he's called on the Congress to pass one of the biggest investments in our defense spending since the days of the Cold War.

And under President Donald Trump, I'll make you a promise: We're going to rebuild our military, we're going to restore the arsenal of democracy, and we are once again going to give our soldiers, sailors, airmen, Marines, and Coast Guard the resources and training they need to accomplish their mission and come home safe. (Applause.)

With the leadership of this Commander-in-Chief, I'm proud to report our armed forces are taking the fight to our enemy on our terms, on their soil. And with President Donald Trump and our brave warriors in the field in Iraq and in Syrian, we will not rest, we will not relent until we hunt down and destroy ISIS at its source, so it can no longer threaten our homeland or threaten our allies around the world. (Applause.)

And when it comes to security at home, our President has been busy as well—securing our borders, enforcing our laws, removing dangerous criminal illegal aliens from our streets, gang members, drug dealers, and violent criminal gangs like MS-13. And I'm pleased to report under President Donald Trump's leadership and the efforts of our Homeland Security, illegal immigrant crossings on our southern border are down more than 60 percent since the first day of 2017. (Applause.)

So President Trump is keeping his promise to make America safe again, and I couldn't be more grateful to serve with him.

But frankly, let me say from my heart how meaningful it is to me to serve with a President who stands without apology for the sanctity of life. (Applause.)

In one of his very first acts in office, President Trump reinstated the Mexico City Policy to keep taxpayer funding out of organizations that perform and promote abortions abroad, and our President has expanded that policy to cover nearly $9 billion in foreign aid. (Applause.)

And President Trump has empowered states to withhold federal funding from abortion providers like Planned Parenthood, and I'm humbled to say that at the President's direction, I was able to cast the tie-breaking vote in Senate to allow states to defund Planned Parenthood. (Applause.)

So this President has been standing for the God-given liberties enshrined in our Constitution. And he's been making sure that his appointments to courts of this land will adhere to the Constitution as it's written, to strictly construe the Constitution. The men and women that we're putting forward to fill our federal benches are going to be people that uphold our highest traditions, like the newest member of Supreme Court of the United States—Justice Neil Gorsuch. (Applause.)

So it's about jobs and prosperity. It's about security at home and abroad. It's our fundamental liberties, and it's strengthening America each and every day. President Trump has done all that and more, and it's been only a little more than six months.

But as the President likes to say, at this White House, that's just what we call a good start. (Applause.)

The truth is we got a lot more work to do. My fellow conservatives, let me assure you: Job one for this administration going forward is we're going to fight every day to keep the promise we made, and we're going to repeal and replace Obamacare. (Applause.)

Last week, it was clear that the Senate wasn't quite ready to keep that promise to the American people, when they fell one vote short of moving forward on a bill to repeal and replace this disastrous policy.

The truth is every day Obamacare survives is another day the American people struggle. When Obamacare passed, we heard a lot of promises. You remember? We heard if you like your doctor, you can keep it—not true. We heard if you like your health insurance, can you keep it—not true. We heard that the cost of health insurance was going to go down. That one sure wasn't true. In fact, we were promised that families would save up to $2,500 in health insurance premiums if this thing became law about seven years ago. And the truth is the average Obamacare plan today costs nearly $3,000 more than a plan did in 2013.

And while premiums are soaring, choices are plummeting. Next year, at least 40 percent of American counties, including nine whole states, will have only one choice of a health insurance provider, meaning they'll essentially have no choice at all.

Even worse, many counties will have no health insurance providers whatsoever in 2018 all across this country. And it's not just about the statistics. It's about real people. It's about small business owners, family farmers all across this country that are struggling to make ends meet.

Behind every number is a name, behind every name is a story. And I've heard these stories as I've traveled across America, and so has the President. Small businesses that talk about the heartache of struggling to keep their whole workforce in place, people that have worked for them for years and years. But with skyrocketing costs of health insurance, they got to choose between keeping the business going and keeping people on the payroll that they've known for years and years.

I've talked to working families—literally a woman in Wisconsin told me that she had to take a pass on paying her health insurance premium for three months just so she'd have enough money to buy Christmas presents for her grandkids.

We all know the truth, America knows the truth: Obamacare has failed and Obamacare must go. (Applause.)

Now, the President and I were disappointed when the Senate came up short in finishing what the House of Representatives had started. In fact, the President said, every single one of those Democrats in the Senate and just a couple—handful of Republicans in his words "let the American people down". And that's the truth of it.

But my fellow conservatives, let me be clear: This ain't over, this ain't by a long shot. (Applause.)

And President Trump—are absolutely committed to keep our promise to the American people. We were not elected to save Obamacare; we were elected to repeal and replace it. And you can know with confidence that President Donald Trump and I are going to fight every day until we end the Obamacare nightmare once and for all. (Applause.)

And when that day comes—and rest assured, it will come—we will begin to restore a healthcare system based on those timeless American principles of personal responsibility, free-market competition, and state-based reform. That's the conservative way to meet the needs of this country in the 21st century when it comes to healthcare, and that is the American way to improve 21st century healthcare for this generation and the next. (Applause.)

And while we're working with this Congress to act on healthcare, I'll make you another promise: President Donald Trump and I are going to roll our sleeves up, sit down with lawmakers, and we're going to pass the largest tax cut since the days of Ronald Reagan.

(Applause.) We're going to cut taxes across the board for working families, small businesses, and family farms.

And President Trump is going cut business taxes in America so American companies can compete with companies around the world to create good-paying jobs right here in gold old USA. (Applause.)

So it's about healthcare. It's about tax cuts. And under this President's leadership, and with the support of this Congress, we're going to keep rolling forward. We'll make those historic investments in national defense to make America stronger and safer than ever before.

We'll keep reining in those unelected bureaucrats so they can't cripple our economy from the comfort of those taxpayer-funded metal desks.

We'll enact real education reform to give families more choices and make it possible for every child to be able to go to the school of their choice and have access to the world-class education every child deserves. It's a lot of work to do.

But I know I'm looking at a lot of young people that are anxious to get to it. So to this rising generation of conservative leaders, I'll tell you—you picked a great time to show up. (Applause.) Because this the moment, now is the time.

To finish what we've started, though, the President and I are counting on all of you. We're counting on this rising generation. We need your voices. We need your values. We need your energy and your vision as never before.

As this rising generation of American leaders, you know that your future, the future of this country depends on what we do in the days ahead. No one has more stake in it than you.

It was President Reagan who memorably said, "Freedom is never more than one generation away from extinction," and this rings just as true today as it did a half century ago when he said it.

So I came here to night really to encourage you to keep standing up. Keep speaking out. Let your voices heard. With your peers and your colleagues, go out there and keep advocating without apology and with cheerfulness the common-sense conservative message that this country longs to hear.

And from this day forward, the President and I are going to have to count on every ounce of your energy. Your enthusiasm, your courage, your conviction, and your passion. And I know we'll have it.

But there's one more thing I might ask of you if you're so inclined. This is a very challenging time in the life of our nation—widening and unknowable threats around the world, too much division here at home, an economy that's now beginning to get on its feet after years of struggling under the weight of big government. And I would just say as you leave here from this great conference energized, hearing all these speakers that you heard this week, you go back to your homes and go back to your schools renewed in your determination to make a difference for conservative values, I'd encourage you if you're inclined to bow the head and bend the knee, it would be a good time to do that, too.

The truth is it's a good time to pray for America because America matters far beyond our shores.

And when I tell you to pray for America, I'm not so much talking about an agenda or a party, but really just pray for this country. Abraham Lincoln I thought had it pretty right. He was asked in his time if he thought God was on his side, and he said, I'd rather concern myself more with whether we're on God's side than whether God is our side.

So just pray for this country. Pray for all who serve her in every capacity because I truly do believe those ancient words of millennia ago are as true today as they've ever been, words that Americans have clung to in much more challenging times than these, that if His people who are called by His name will humble themselves and pray, he'll hear from Heaven, and he'll heal this land, this one nation, under God, indivisible, with liberty and justice for all. (Applause.)

AUDIENCE: USA! USA! USA!

THE VICE PRESIDENT: So in a word, men and women of the Young America's Foundation, have faith. Have faith in the principles that you hold in your hearts that brought you to this place today. Have faith in each other, and in your fellow conservatives, the ability to make a difference as conservatives have ever since this movement was born. Have faith in this President, who I promise you and the whole team is fighting for you every. And above all else, have a boundless faith in the American people, and in Him who placed this miracle of democracy on this wilderness shores, that He will still do as He's always done, He will bless America.

And so I say to this rising generation, with your support, with the leadership that we have in President Donald Trump and in our majorities in the House and Senate and all across this land, and with all of your shining faces, I'm confident, together, we will make America safe again. Together, we will make America prosperous again. And together, to borrow a phrase, we will Make America Great Again.

Thank you very much. God bless the Young America's Foundation and God bless the United States of America. (Applause.)

END

Source: Remarks by the Vice President to the Young America's Foundation. (2017, August 4). Retrieved January 29, 2018, from https://www.whitehouse.gov/briefings-statements/remarks-vice-president-young-americas-foundation/.

3. Below is a list of sentences that contain partial quotes. On the basis of the rationale outlined in the chapter, determine if the partial quote has value, and explain why you think that way.

- Judge Albert Thames ruled that Lynne Flabeau should spend the rest of her life in prison for killing her roommate in a "vomit-inducing fashion."

- The president said he would "in no way" allow the Senate bill to become law.

- CBS commentator Billy Packer was condemned in the media after he referred to basketball player Allen Iverson as a "tough monkey."

- Superintendent Jarious Watkins said he planned to "figure out" how more than a dozen teachers had helped students cheat on the state's performance-evaluation test.

- Football coach Herman Ruth said his team's opponent on Saturday is "slow as a dead turtle," noting that he planned to savor an easy victory.

- In a war of words before the mayoral debate, challenger Richie Magnus said his opponent, the sitting mayor, "be stupid dumb."

- After visiting the Louvre, the student said the artwork there was "impressive" and "quite beautiful."

4. Interview a person of interest to you. Take notes on the interview for the purpose of gathering direct and indirect quotes. (Feel free to record it, if you want.) Then, write a two-page "story" about what this person told you, relying entirely on the paraphrase-quote

structure outlined in the book. Remember, you need to organize the piece so that it moves smoothly from chunk to chunk, and the story needs to start with what you think is most important and move to what you think is least important.

5. Research a meeting and write an expanded inverted-pyramid story about it. Prepare for the event by obtaining a copy of the agenda and researching the event. In advance of the meeting, call at least one source to help you find out what important developments might occur or what important votes might take place. Then, attend the meeting and gather the material you need to write the story. You will want a strong lead and a good bridge. You should be able to create background paragraphs from the research you conducted in advance. Then, build the rest of the piece out of paraphrases and quotes.

6. Analyze the pros and cons associated with fixing people's direct quotes. You can use those noted in the chapter as well as any others you think apply. In what circumstances do you see yourself feeling the need to change quotes, and in what cases would you do so? Is there any case in which you absolutely would not change someone's quotes? Write a reflection essay on this issue.

WRITING FOR BROADCAST

REVIEW

1. What does the abbreviation "KISS" mean, and how does it apply to broadcast writing?

2. The chapter states that broadcast writing is done "for the ear." What does that mean, and how do you write in that fashion?

3. How does an inverted-pyramid lead differ from a broadcast lead? What is it about broadcast journalism that makes this difference necessary?

4. What is a pronouncer, and how does it help a broadcaster?

5. What does the term "wallpaper" mean in a broadcast context? How can you write a script to avoid this problem?

6. What are the five broadcast story formats discussed in this chapter? Explain each of them in one or two sentences.

7. To finish polishing up your package, what does the chapter say are four things you should check before declaring that you are done with your work?

WRITING EXERCISES

1. Watch a local nightly newscast and keep track of how many of the five types of stories listed in the chapter the newscast uses. Which ones are dominant, and which ones have lesser or no representation? Why do you think this is? Write a short essay that outlines your findings and justifies your thoughts regarding the newscast.

2. Find five words or terms you would use locally that you think might be problematic for people outside your area. These could be names of people and places or abbreviations and acronyms. Write a sentence that includes each word as well as a properly structured pronouncer.

3. Below are words that could easily be mispronounced. Research the terms and write a pronouncer for each of them. Make sure to use hyphens to separate the syllables and capital letters to show emphasis.
    *   The musical artist "Sade"
    *   U.S. Congresswoman Amata Coleman Radewagen
    *   Colonel
    *   Phlegm
    *   Haleiwa, Hawaii
    *   Vince Papale

4. Below are sentences that need to be rewritten for broadcast style. Consider using strong noun-verb-object structure, trimming unneeded words and using words that add sound and feel to them as you write for the ear. Also, review the section on numbers, symbols, acronyms and other readability issues so you can apply those suggestions here:
    a. Approximately 12.2 inches of snow fell upon Chicago in less than 24 hours, creating a blizzard that led to at least 341 minor traffic crashes during the 5 p.m. drive time.

b. The St. Louis Cardinals were defeated by the Milwaukee Brewers when Ryan Braun hit a ninth-inning home run very far into the bleachers in right field.

c. The St. Paul Foundation was found to have an administrator, Bill Jackson, who illegally took $1,401,082 from the church's rain-day fund.

d. Freddie Middlebrook of 821 E. 121st St. in Oconomowoc was formally accused of shooting a coworker named Gene Agnew to death over a debt of $9.89.

e. To take part in WTRV-TV's 8 a.m. discussion on social media, you should send a text message to 83424 and include #CHATUP.

5. The book notes the pros and cons of using the term "you" in broadcast journalism. Given your own experiences with viewing broadcast and your own sense of journalism, do you think using second person is effective in this form of writing? Defend your answer.

6. Here is the information on the fire included earlier in the workbook. Write a 20-second reader in broadcast format. Be sure to include a broadcast-style lead and a solid close. Then, record yourself voicing the reader and listen to the final product. If you find the recording is too long or you made errors with regard to word choices, go back and edit your copy and revoice the reader. Finally, compare and contrast your final copy from the inverted-pyramid exercise with the reader you completed for this assignment. Be sure to examine length, structure and word choice in your analysis of your work.

Source: Lt. Sam Sires, Beacontown Fire Department

INFORMATION: The Beacontown Fire Department responded to a call around 2 a.m. Wednesday of a potential fire in the area of Broadway and Fifth Avenue. Chief's Car 6, Pumper Truck 5, Engine Company 8 and other support vehicles responded as a result. Firefighters arrived at 1002 N. Fifth Ave. to find the one-story, three-bedroom home fully enveloped in flames. The homeowners, Wendy Walther and Zeke Walther, were outside of the home, as was their daughter, Fiona. No one was left inside. Nobody was injured.

Firefighters deployed several hose lines and fought the blaze for five hours until getting full control of the situation. Two fire marshals eventually were able to enter the remains of the home to determine the cause of the blaze. They stated that the fire began when a space heater tipped over in the living room and ignited a couch. The fire then spread along the room's ceiling, which consisted mostly of very old wood.

The home is considered a total loss, and the loss is estimated to be $300,000 in damages.

7. Here is the information on the health-related concerns included earlier in the workbook. Write a 40-second VO/SOT in broadcast format. Be sure to include a broadcast-style lead

and a solid close. For the soundbite, you may use any chunk of the text below as if the source had said it directly to you on tape. (The soundbite should be somewhere between 8 and 12 seconds.) List what you would consider to be valuable b-roll that would cover your voice track if you had the opportunity to shoot video. Be sure to examine length, structure and word choice in your analysis of your work.

Source: Melanie Danbury, head of the University of Springfield's student health center

INFORMATION: Last week, we began receiving reports that several students in the residence halls were becoming ill. Around that time, we also had seen an increase in walk-in traffic at the health center. The students in the residence halls and those students who came to our offices complained of stomach cramps, diarrhea and vomiting. Some students had also become massively dehydrated as a result of these symptoms. Those students were taken to University Hospital for treatment.

We collected several forms of samples from these individuals and found a common thread in their illness. These students were suffering from Escherichia bacterial poisoning, more commonly known as E. coli poisoning. As we worked our way through the treatment of these students, we began to experience a continuing stream of students with similar symptoms entering the health center. They, too, were tested for and found to have E. coli poisoning.

After conducting interviews with as many of the patients as possible, we were able to determine that all of the individuals had been eating frequently at Bob's Café, the food-service eatery within the Nelson Residence Hall Complex. In addition, they all noted consuming some form of meat from the café. We immediately reached out to the university's food staff and closed Bob's Café until further notice as we conducted an investigation of this potential contagion.

Today, we are releasing the results of our report. It appears that a refrigeration unit at Bob's Café had broken down, leaving the meat within that unit at an unsafe temperature. It is our finding that E. coli bacteria spread throughout the meat in that unit and has led to this outbreak of illness.

Students who have eaten at Bob's Café, especially those with weakened immune systems and those who ate meat frequently over the past week, should immediately come to the health center for examination. If you note the presence of any of these symptoms, regardless of where you have been eating, contact the health center immediately. To prevent the spread of this illness, students should wash their hands frequently as well as wash any utensils and food-serving items. We have also set up a page on the university's website to answer any additional questions you may have.

PUBLIC RELATIONS

REVIEW

1. What are five terms listed in your chapter that appear in many good definitions of public relations?

2. Explain the purpose of a news release, and then list a few basic types of news releases.

3. Why is transparency important in public relations?

4. What is the difference between an internal and an external audience?

5. Why is it important to work with the news media as a public relations practitioner?

WRITING EXERCISES

1. Below is a list of jargon-filled sentences. Examine each sentence and come up with a more common way to say each of them.

    - We experienced a four-quarter financial downturn for our corporation.

    - Smith Corporation regretfully announces the shedding of 230 members of our frontline workforce.

    - Despite the best efforts of our surgical team, we completed the task with a negative patient outcome of the highest order.

    - According to our financial ledgers, our organization's chief financial officer has been engaged in unauthorized financial transfers for personal gain without our knowledge for at least the past 36 months.

    - The new engine in the Ford Mustang places it at the front of all high-performance vehicles in terms of speed when accelerating from a dead stop to 60 miles per hour.

    - We understand that we knowingly engaged in disinformation with the general public.

2. Download a press release from an organization that interests you, and compare its formatting structure to that of the Lindsey + Asp release in the book. What elements are present, and which elements are missing? What elements are present but differ slightly, such as a headline not written in bold or capital letters? Does the release you downloaded contain any additional elements that you find helpful or valuable? In comparing and contrasting the releases, which one is easier to understand? Also, how well does it do in supporting its claims, acting in a transparent fashion and presenting the information clearly? Write a short essay that explains your experience.

3. Select a public relations agency that has established a social media presence on a platform you use frequently. Track that organization's use of social media over the course of a week. How often and when does the group post? What items are posted most frequently, and are they effectively communicated to the audiences for this firm? Does the group follow the 70/20/10 approach outlined in the social media chapter? In your opinion, does this organization use social media effectively? Why or why not? Write a short essay on your findings.

4. Below is the same information about the health-related issue used elsewhere in this book, with a few alterations. Use this information to write a one- or two-page "bad

news" release with your campus community, especially the student community, being the main audience for this. You need to announce the most important information in a transparent and straightforward fashion, but you also don't want to create a panic. Then compare and contrast this with the brief you wrote earlier, and write a short reflective essay on your work on both of these writing experiences.

Source: Melanie Danbury, head of the university's student health center

INFORMATION: Last week, we began receiving reports that several students in the residence halls were becoming ill. Around that time, we also had seen an increase in walk-in traffic at the health center. The students in the residence halls and those students who came to our offices complained of stomach cramps, diarrhea and vomiting. Some students had also become massively dehydrated as a result of these symptoms. Those students were taken to University Hospital for treatment.

We collected several forms of samples from these individuals and found a common thread in their illness. These students were suffering from Escherichia bacterial poisoning, more commonly known as E. coli poisoning. As we worked our way through the treatment of these students, we began to experience a continued stream of students with similar symptoms entering the health center. They, too, were tested for and found to have E. coli poisoning.

After conducting interviews with as many of the patients as possible, we were able to determine that all of the individuals had been eating frequently at [FILL IN THE NAME OF YOUR PRIMARY RESIDENCE HALL AND EATING VENUE]. In addition, they all noted consuming some form of meat from the café. We immediately reached out to the university's food staff and closed this food outlet until further notice as we conducted an investigation of this potential contagion.

Today, we are releasing the results of our report. It appears that a refrigeration unit had broken down, leaving the meat within that unit at an unsafe temperature. It is our finding that E. coli bacteria spread throughout the meat in that unit and has led to this outbreak of illness.

Students who have eaten at this on-campus eatery, especially those with weakened immune systems and those who ate meat frequently over the past week, should immediately come to the health center for examination. If you note the presence of any of these symptoms, regardless of where you have been eating, contact the health center immediately. To prevent the spread of this illness, students should wash their hands frequently as well as wash any utensils and food-serving items. We have also set up a page on the university's website to answer any additional questions you may have.

5. Below is the transcript of President Donald Trump's 2017 joint address to Congress. Use the content here to craft a two-page news release as if you were a member of the president's public relations staff. Use your own contact information for the identification block and follow the formatting approach described in the book for other key structural elements. Feel free to conduct an internet search for any information you would like to include as background on Trump or for the boilerplate information at the end.

U.S. Capitol
Washington, D.C.
9:09 p.m. EST

THE PRESIDENT: Thank you very much. Mr. Speaker, Mr. Vice President, members of Congress, the First Lady of the United States—(applause)—and citizens of America:

Tonight, as we mark the conclusion of our celebration of Black History Month, we are reminded of our nation's path towards civil rights and the work that still remains to be done. (Applause.) Recent threats targeting Jewish community centers and vandalism of Jewish cemeteries, as well as last week's shooting in Kansas City, remind us that while we may be a nation divided on policies, we are a country that stands united in condemning hate and evil in all of its very ugly forms. (Applause.)

Each American generation passes the torch of truth, liberty and justice in an unbroken chain all the way down to the present. That torch is now in our hands. And we will use it to light up the world. I am here tonight to deliver a message of unity and strength, and it is a message deeply delivered from my heart. A new chapter—(applause)—of American Greatness is now beginning. A new national pride is sweeping across our nation. And a new surge of optimism is placing impossible dreams firmly within our grasp.

What we are witnessing today is the renewal of the American spirit. Our allies will find that America is once again ready to lead. (Applause.) All the nations of the world—friend or foe—will find that America is strong, America is proud, and America is free.

In nine years, the United States will celebrate the 250th anniversary of our founding—250 years since the day we declared our independence. It will be one of the great milestones in the history of the world. But what will America look like as we reach our 250th year? What kind of country will we leave for our children?

I will not allow the mistakes of recent decades past to define the course of our future. For too long, we've watched our middle class shrink as we've exported our jobs and wealth to foreign countries. We've financed and built one global project after another, but ignored the fates of our children in the inner cities of Chicago, Baltimore, Detroit, and so many other places throughout our land.

We've defended the borders of other nations while leaving our own borders wide open for anyone to cross and for drugs to pour in at a now unprecedented rate. And we've spent trillions and trillions of dollars overseas, while our infrastructure at home has so badly crumbled.

Then, in 2016, the Earth shifted beneath our feet. The rebellion started as a quiet protest, spoken by families of all colors and creeds—families who just wanted a fair shot for their children and a fair hearing for their concerns.

But then the quiet voices became a loud chorus as thousands of citizens now spoke out together, from cities small and large, all across our country. Finally, the chorus became an earthquake, and the people turned out by the tens of millions, and they were all united by one very simple, but crucial demand: that America must put its own citizens first. Because only then can we truly make America great again. (Applause.)

Dying industries will come roaring back to life. Heroic veterans will get the care they so desperately need. Our military will be given the resources its brave warriors so richly deserve. Crumbling infrastructure will be replaced with new roads, bridges, tunnels, airports and railways gleaming across our very, very beautiful land. Our terrible drug epidemic will slow down and, ultimately, stop. And our neglected inner cities will see a rebirth of hope, safety and opportunity. Above all else, we will keep our promises to the American people. (Applause.)

It's been a little over a month since my inauguration, and I want to take this moment to update the nation on the progress I've made in keeping those promises.

Since my election, Ford, Fiat-Chrysler, General Motors, Sprint, Softbank, Lockheed, Intel, Walmart and many others have announced that they will invest billions and billions of dollars in the United States, and will create tens of thousands of new American jobs. (Applause.)

The stock market has gained almost $3 trillion in value since the election on November 8th, a record. We've saved taxpayers hundreds of millions of dollars by bringing down the price of a fantastic—and it is a fantastic—new F-35 jet fighter, and we'll be saving billions more on contracts all across our government. We have placed a hiring freeze on non-military and non-essential federal workers.

We have begun to drain the swamp of government corruption by imposing a five-year ban on lobbying by executive branch officials and a lifetime ban—(applause)—thank you—and a lifetime ban on becoming lobbyists for a foreign government.

We have undertaken a historic effort to massively reduce job-crushing regulations, creating a deregulation task force inside of every government agency. (Applause.) And we're imposing a new rule which mandates that for every one new regulation, two old regulations must be eliminated. (Applause.) We're going to stop the regulations that threaten the future and livelihood of our great coal miners. (Applause.)

We have cleared the way for the construction of the Keystone and Dakota Access Pipelines—(applause)—thereby creating tens of thousands of jobs. And I've issued a new directive that new American pipelines be made with American steel. (Applause.)

We have withdrawn the United States from the job-killing Trans-Pacific Partnership. (Applause.) And with the help of Prime Minister Justin Trudeau, we have formed a council with our neighbors in Canada to help ensure that women entrepreneurs have access to the networks, markets and capital they need to start a business and live out their financial dreams. (Applause.)

To protect our citizens, I have directed the Department of Justice to form a Task Force on Reducing Violent Crime. I have further ordered the Departments of Homeland Security and Justice, along with the Department of State and the Director of National Intelligence, to coordinate an aggressive strategy to dismantle the criminal cartels that have spread all across our nation. (Applause.) We will stop the drugs from pouring into our country and poisoning our youth, and we will expand treatment for those who have become so badly addicted. (Applause.)

At the same time, my administration has answered the pleas of the American people for immigration enforcement and border security. (Applause.) By finally enforcing our immigration laws, we will raise wages, help the unemployed, save billions and billions of dollars, and make our communities safer for everyone. (Applause.) We want all Americans to succeed, but that can't happen in an environment of lawless chaos. We must restore integrity and the rule of law at our borders. (Applause.)

For that reason, we will soon begin the construction of a great, great wall along our southern border. (Applause.) As we speak tonight, we are removing gang members, drug dealers, and criminals that threaten our communities and prey on our very innocent citizens. Bad ones are going out as I speak, and as I promised throughout the campaign.

To any in Congress who do not believe we should enforce our laws, I would ask you this one question: What would you say to the American family that loses their jobs, their income, or their loved one because America refused to uphold its laws and defend its borders? (Applause.)

Our obligation is to serve, protect, and defend the citizens of the United States. We are also taking strong measures to protect our nation from radical Islamic terrorism. (Applause.) According to data provided by the Department of Justice, the vast majority of individuals convicted of terrorism and terrorism-related offenses since 9/11 came here from outside of our country. We have seen the attacks at home—from Boston to San Bernardino to the Pentagon, and, yes, even the World Trade Center.

We have seen the attacks in France, in Belgium, in Germany, and all over the world. It is not compassionate, but reckless to allow uncontrolled entry from places where proper vetting cannot occur. (Applause.) Those given the high honor of admission to the United States should support this country and love its people and its values. We cannot allow a beachhead of terrorism to form inside America. We cannot allow our nation to become a sanctuary for extremists. (Applause.)

That is why my administration has been working on improved vetting procedures, and we will shortly take new steps to keep our nation safe and to keep out those out who will do us harm. (Applause.)

As promised, I directed the Department of Defense to develop a plan to demolish and destroy ISIS—a network of lawless savages that have slaughtered Muslims and Christians, and men, and women, and children of all faiths and all beliefs. We will work with our allies, including our friends and allies in the Muslim world, to extinguish this vile enemy from our planet. (Applause.)

I have also imposed new sanctions on entities and individuals who support Iran's ballistic missile program, and reaffirmed our unbreakable alliance with the State of Israel. (Applause.)

Finally, I have kept my promise to appoint a justice to the United States Supreme Court, from my list of 20 judges, who will defend our Constitution. (Applause.)

I am greatly honored to have Maureen Scalia with us in the gallery tonight. (Applause.) Thank you, Maureen. Her late, great husband, Antonin Scalia, will forever be a symbol of American justice. To fill his seat, we have chosen Judge Neil Gorsuch, a man of incredible skill and deep devotion to the law. He was confirmed unanimously by the Court of Appeals, and I am asking the Senate to swiftly approve his nomination. (Applause.)

Tonight, as I outline the next steps we must take as a country, we must honestly acknowledge the circumstances we inherited. Ninety-four million Americans are out of the labor force. Over 43 million people are now living in poverty, and over 43 million Americans are on food stamps. More than one in five people in their prime working years are not working. We have the worst financial recovery in 65 years. In the last eight years, the past administration has put on more new debt than nearly all of the other Presidents combined.

We've lost more than one-fourth of our manufacturing jobs since NAFTA was approved, and we've lost 60,000 factories since China joined the World Trade Organization in 2001. Our trade deficit in goods with the world last year was nearly $800 billion dollars. And overseas we have inherited a series of tragic foreign policy disasters.

Solving these and so many other pressing problems will require us to work past the differences of party. It will require us to tap into the American spirit that has overcome every challenge throughout our long and storied history. But to accomplish our goals at home and abroad, we must restart the engine of the American economy—making it easier for companies to do business in the United States, and much, much harder for companies to leave our country. (Applause.)

Right now, American companies are taxed at one of the highest rates anywhere in the world. My economic team is developing historic tax reform that will reduce the tax rate on our companies so they can compete and thrive anywhere and with anyone. (Applause.) It will be a big, big cut.

At the same time, we will provide massive tax relief for the middle class. We must create a level playing field for American companies and our workers. We have to do it. (Applause.) Currently, when we ship products out of America, many other countries make us pay very high tariffs and taxes. But when foreign companies ship their products into America, we charge them nothing, or almost nothing.

I just met with officials and workers from a great American company, Harley-Davidson. In fact, they proudly displayed five of their magnificent motorcycles, made in the USA, on the front lawn of the White House. ((Laughter and applause.) And they wanted me to ride one and I said, "No, thank you." (Laughter.)

At our meeting, I asked them, how are you doing, how is business? They said that it's good. I asked them further, how are you doing with other countries, mainly international sales? They told me—without even complaining, because they have been so mistreated for so long that they've become used to it—that it's very hard to do business with other countries because they tax our goods at such a high rate. They said that in the case of another country, they taxed their motorcycles at 100 percent. They weren't even asking for a change. But I am. (Applause.)

I believe strongly in free trade but it also has to be fair trade. It's been a long time since we had fair trade. The first Republican President, Abraham Lincoln, warned that the "abandonment of the protective policy by the American government…will produce want and ruin among our people." Lincoln was right—and it's time we heeded his advice and his words. (Applause.) I am not going to let America and its great companies and workers be taken advantage of us any longer. They have taken advantage of our country. No longer. (Applause.)

I am going to bring back millions of jobs. Protecting our workers also means reforming our system of legal immigration. (Applause.) The current, outdated system depresses wages for our poorest workers, and puts great pressure on taxpayers. Nations around the world, like Canada, Australia and many others, have a merit-based immigration system. (Applause.) It's a basic principle that those seeking to enter a country ought to be able to support themselves financially. Yet, in America, we do not enforce this rule, straining the very public resources that our poorest citizens rely upon. According to the National Academy of Sciences, our current immigration system costs American taxpayers many billions of dollars a year.

Switching away from this current system of lower-skilled immigration, and instead adopting a merit-based system, we will have so many more benefits. It will save countless dollars, raise workers' wages, and help struggling families—including immigrant families—enter the middle class. And they will do it quickly, and they will be very, very happy, indeed. (Applause.)

I believe that real and positive immigration reform is possible, as long as we focus on the following goals: To improve jobs and wages for Americans; to strengthen our nation's security; and to restore respect for our laws. If we are guided by the wellbeing of American citizens, then I believe Republicans and Democrats can work together to achieve an outcome that has eluded our country for decades. (Applause.)

Another Republican President, Dwight D. Eisenhower, initiated the last truly great national infrastructure program—the building of the Interstate Highway System. The time has come for a new program of national rebuilding. (Applause.) America has spent approximately $6 trillion in the Middle East—all the while our infrastructure at home is crumbling. With this $6 trillion, we could have rebuilt our country twice, and maybe even three times if we had people who had the ability to negotiate. (Applause.)

To launch our national rebuilding, I will be asking Congress to approve legislation that produces a $1 trillion investment in infrastructure of the United States—financed through both public and private capital—creating millions of new jobs. (Applause.) This effort will be guided by two core principles: buy American and hire American. (Applause.)

Tonight, I am also calling on this Congress to repeal and replace Obamacare—(applause)—with reforms that expand choice, increase access, lower costs, and, at the same time, provide better healthcare. (Applause.)

Mandating every American to buy government-approved health insurance was never the right solution for our country. (Applause.) The way to make health insurance available to everyone is to lower the cost of health insurance, and that is what we are going do. (Applause.)

Obamacare premiums nationwide have increased by double and triple digits. As an example, Arizona went up 116 percent last year alone. Governor Matt Bevin of Kentucky just said Obamacare is failing in his state—the state of Kentucky—and it's unsustainable and collapsing.

One-third of counties have only one insurer, and they are losing them fast. They are losing them so fast. They are leaving, and many Americans have no choice at all. There's no choice left. Remember when you were told that you could keep your doctor and keep your plan? We now know that all of those promises have been totally broken. Obamacare is collapsing, and we must act decisively to protect all Americans. (Applause.)

Action is not a choice, it is a necessity. So I am calling on all Democrats and Republicans in Congress to work with us to save Americans from this imploding Obamacare disaster. (Applause.)

Here are the principles that should guide the Congress as we move to create a better healthcare system for all Americans:

First, we should ensure that Americans with preexisting conditions have access to coverage, and that we have a stable transition for Americans currently enrolled in the healthcare exchanges. (Applause.)

Secondly, we should help Americans purchase their own coverage through the use of tax credits and expanded Health Savings Accounts—but it must be the plan they want, not the plan forced on them by our government. (Applause.)

Thirdly, we should give our great state governors the resources and flexibility they need with Medicaid to make sure no one is left out. (Applause.)

Fourth, we should implement legal reforms that protect patients and doctors from unnecessary costs that drive up the price of insurance, and work to bring down the artificially high price of drugs, and bring them down immediately. (Applause.)

And finally, the time has come to give Americans the freedom to purchase health insurance across state lines—(applause)—which will create a truly competitive national marketplace that will bring costs way down and provide far better care. So important.

Everything that is broken in our country can be fixed. Every problem can be solved. And every hurting family can find healing and hope.

Our citizens deserve this, and so much more—so why not join forces and finally get the job done, and get it done right? (Applause.) On this and so many other things, Democrats and Republicans should get together and unite for the good of our country and for the good of the American people. (Applause.)

My administration wants to work with members of both parties to make childcare accessible and affordable, to help ensure new parents that they have paid family leave—(applause)—to invest in women's health, and to promote clean air and clean water, and to rebuild our military and our infrastructure. (Applause.)

True love for our people requires us to find common ground, to advance the common good, and to cooperate on behalf of every American child who deserves a much brighter future.

An incredible young woman is with us this evening, who should serve as an inspiration to us all. Today is Rare Disease Day, and joining us in the gallery is a rare disease survivor, Megan Crowley. (Applause.)

Megan was diagnosed with Pompe disease, a rare and serious illness, when she was 15 months old. She was not expected to live past five. On receiving this news, Megan's dad, John, fought with everything he had to save the life of his precious child. He founded a company to look for a cure, and helped develop the drug that saved Megan's life. Today she is 20 years old and a sophomore at Notre Dame. (Applause.)

Megan's story is about the unbounded power of a father's love for a daughter. But our slow and burdensome approval process at the Food and Drug Administration keeps too many advances, like the one that saved Megan's life, from reaching those in need. If we slash the restraints, not just at the FDA but across our government, then we will be blessed with far more miracles just like Megan. (Applause.) In fact, our children will grow up in a nation of miracles.

But to achieve this future, we must enrich the mind and the souls of every American child. Education is the civil rights issue of our time. (Applause.) I am calling upon members of both parties to pass an education bill that funds school choice for disadvantaged youth, including millions of African American and Latino children. (Applause.) These families should be free to choose the public, private, charter, magnet, religious, or home school that is right for them. (Applause.)

Joining us tonight in the gallery is a remarkable woman, Denisha Merriweather. As a young girl, Denisha struggled in school and failed third grade twice. But then she was able to enroll in a private center for learning—a great learning center—with the help of a tax credit and a scholarship program.

Today, she is the first in her family to graduate, not just from high school, but from college. Later this year she will get her master's degree in social work. We want all children to be able to break the cycle of poverty just like Denisha. (Applause.)

But to break the cycle of poverty, we must also break the cycle of violence. The murder rate in 2015 experienced its largest single-year increase in nearly half a century. In Chicago, more than 4,000 people were shot last year alone, and the murder rate so far this year has been even higher. This is not acceptable in our society. (Applause.)

Every American child should be able to grow up in a safe community, to attend a great school, and to have access to a high-paying job. (Applause.) But to create this future, we must work with, not against—not against—the men and women of law enforcement. (Applause.) We must build bridges of cooperation and trust—not drive the wedge of disunity and, really, it's what it is, division. It's pure, unadulterated division. We have to unify.

Police and sheriffs are members of our community. They're friends and neighbors, they're mothers and fathers, sons and daughters—and they leave behind loved ones every day who worry about whether or not they'll come home safe and sound. We must support the incredible men and women of law enforcement. (Applause.)

And we must support the victims of crime. I have ordered the Department of Homeland Security to create an office to serve American victims. The office is called VOICE—Victims of Immigration Crime Engagement. We are providing a voice to those who have been ignored by our media and silenced by special interests. (Applause.) Joining us in the audience tonight are four very brave Americans whose government failed them. Their names are Jamiel Shaw, Susan Oliver, Jenna Oliver, and Jessica Davis.

Jamiel's 17-year-old son was viciously murdered by an illegal immigrant gang member who had just been released from prison. Jamiel Shaw, Jr. was an incredible young man, with unlimited potential who was getting ready to go to college where he would have excelled as a great college quarterback. But he never got the chance. His father, who is in the audience tonight, has become a very good friend of mine. Jamiel, thank you. Thank you. (Applause.)

Also with us are Susan Oliver and Jessica Davis. Their husbands, Deputy Sheriff Danny Oliver and Detective Michael Davis, were slain in the line of duty in California. They were pillars of their community. These brave men were viciously gunned down by an illegal immigrant with a criminal record and two prior deportations. Should have never been in our country.

Sitting with Susan is her daughter, Jenna. Jenna, I want you to know that your father was a hero, and that tonight you have the love of an entire country supporting you and praying for you. (Applause.)

To Jamiel, Jenna, Susan and Jessica, I want you to know that we will never stop fighting for justice. Your loved ones will never, ever be forgotten. We will always honor their memory. (Applause.)

Finally, to keep America safe, we must provide the men and women of the United States military with the tools they need to prevent war—if they must—they have to fight and they only have to win. (Applause.)

I am sending Congress a budget that rebuilds the military, eliminates the defense sequester—(applause)—and calls for one of the largest increases in national defense spending in American history. My budget will also increase funding for our veterans. Our veterans have delivered for this nation, and now we must deliver for them. (Applause.)

The challenges we face as a nation are great, but our people are even greater. And none are greater or braver than those who fight for America in uniform. (Applause.)

We are blessed to be joined tonight by Carryn Owens, the widow of a U.S. Navy Special Operator, Senior Chief William "Ryan" Owens. Ryan died as he lived: a warrior and a hero, battling against terrorism and securing our nation. (Applause.) I just spoke to our great General Mattis, just now, who reconfirmed that—and I quote—"Ryan was a part of a highly successful raid that generated large amounts of vital intelligence that will lead to many more victories in the future against our enemies." Ryan's legacy is etched into eternity. Thank you. (Applause.) And Ryan is looking down, right now—you know that—and he is very happy because I think he just broke a record. (Laughter and applause.)

For as the Bible teaches us, "There is no greater act of love than to lay down one's life for one's friends." Ryan laid down his life for his friends, for his country, and for our freedom. And we will never forget Ryan. (Applause.)

To those allies who wonder what kind of a friend America will be, look no further than the heroes who wear our uniform. Our foreign policy calls for a direct, robust and meaningful engagement with the world. It is American leadership based on vital security interests that we share with our allies all across the globe.

We strongly support NATO, an alliance forged through the bonds of two world wars that dethroned fascism, and a Cold War, and defeated communism. (Applause.)

But our partners must meet their financial obligations. And now, based on our very strong and frank discussions, they are beginning to do just that. In fact, I can tell you, the money is pouring in. Very nice. (Applause.) We expect our partners—whether in NATO, the Middle East, or in the Pacific—to take a direct and meaningful role in both strategic and military operations, and pay their fair share of the cost. Have to do that.

We will respect historic institutions, but we will respect the foreign rights of all nations, and they have to respect our rights as a nation also. (Applause.) Free nations are the best vehicle for expressing the will of the people, and America respects the right of all nations to chart their own path. My job is not to represent the world. My job is to represent the United States of America. (Applause.)

But we know that America is better off when there is less conflict, not more. We must learn from the mistakes of the past. We have seen the war and the destruction that have ravaged and raged throughout the world—all across the world. The only long-term solution for these humanitarian disasters, in many cases, is to create the conditions where displaced persons can safely return home and begin the long, long process of rebuilding. (Applause.)

America is willing to find new friends, and to forge new partnerships, where shared interests align. We want harmony and stability, not war and conflict. We want peace, wherever peace can be found.

America is friends today with former enemies. Some of our closest allies, decades ago, fought on the opposite side of these terrible, terrible wars. This history should give us all faith in the possibilities for a better world. Hopefully, the 250th year for America will see a world that is more peaceful, more just, and more free.

On our 100th anniversary, in 1876, citizens from across our nation came to Philadelphia to celebrate America's centennial. At that celebration, the country's builders and artists and inventors showed off their wonderful creations. Alexander Graham Bell displayed his telephone for the first time. Remington unveiled the first typewriter. An early attempt was made at electric light. Thomas Edison showed an automatic telegraph and an electric pen. Imagine the wonders our country could know in America's 250th year. (Applause.)

Think of the marvels we can achieve if we simply set free the dreams of our people. Cures to the illnesses that have always plagued us are not too much to hope. American footprints on distant worlds are not too big a dream. Millions lifted from welfare to work is not too much to expect. And streets where mothers are safe from fear, schools where children learn in peace, and jobs where Americans prosper and grow are not too much to ask. (Applause.)

When we have all of this, we will have made America greater than ever before—for all Americans. This is our vision. This is our mission. But we can only get there together. We are one people, with one destiny. We all bleed the same blood. We all salute the same great American flag. And we all are made by the same God. (Applause.)

When we fulfill this vision, when we celebrate our 250 years of glorious freedom, we will look back on tonight as when this new chapter of American Greatness began. The time for small thinking is over. The time for trivial fights is behind us. We just need the courage to share the dreams that fill our hearts, the bravery to express the hopes that stir our souls, and the confidence to turn those hopes and those dreams into action.

From now on, America will be empowered by our aspirations, not burdened by our fears; inspired by the future, not bound by the failures of the past; and guided by our vision, not blinded by our doubts.

I am asking all citizens to embrace this renewal of the American spirit. I am asking all members of Congress to join me in dreaming big, and bold, and daring things for our country. I am asking everyone watching tonight to seize this moment. Believe in yourselves, believe in your future, and believe, once more, in America.

Thank you, God bless you, and God bless the United States. (Applause.)

END
10:09 p.m. EST

Source: Remarks by President Donald Trump in Joint Address to Congress. (2017, February 28). Retrieved January 29, 2018, from https://www.whitehouse.gov/briefings-statements/remarks-president-trump-joint-address-congress/.

6. Research an upcoming event at your school, and create a one-page fact sheet on it. Use the formatting in the book for the fact sheet, and make sure to include an information block and other key elements associated with this type of release. The type of event will dictate what facts you include, but you should have at least one block of information that answers the 5W's and 1H of the event, one set of bulleted facts and one paragraph of information that offers a more detailed explanation of a key aspect of the event or the group's reason for hosting it.

7. Using the information below, craft a two-page announcement press release for your school. (If your school's head position is a president instead of a chancellor, feel free to use those terms interchangeably in the content as you rewrite it for your release.) Follow the format for the announcement release used in the chapter. Consider the audience for this release to be your campus community as well as the surrounding area. Keep in mind you should check the material below for AP style errors, as not all material you will receive in your job will automatically be in the proper style. Make sure to attribute information to sources if you are quoting individuals or using opinion-based content.

Due to family obligations, our previous chancellor resigned on June 30. He returned to Georgia where he will become the provost at the University of Georgia.

A search committee of 4 administrators, 4 faculty and 4 students spent the next several months reviewing a pool of more than 200 potential candidates. A group of five finalists was drawn from that pool. Of the five finalists, two candidates withdrew. Of the remaining three, one candidate was agreed upon by all 12 committee members after an exhaustive set of telephone and campus interviews.

Today, the finalist agreed to terms and has signed a contract.

James Newcastle will be the next chancellor of this institution, starting this coming September 1.

- He is 49 years old.

- He is married to his wife, Beth. They have two sons: Bob (21) and Bill (25).

- His last job was as provost at West Northeastern University in Fargo, North Dakota, where he served for four years. He has also been the chairman of the department of communications at Indiana State University, where he was also a faculty member for a total of 12 years.

- He has BA in journalism from the University of Missouri. He has a master's degree in psychology from Stanford University. He has a Ph.D. in communications from the University of Texas.

- He served terms as the National Communication Association president and vice president. He has also served on more than a dozen state and regional communication association boards of directors.

- He lives in Fargo, North Dakota, but plans to relocate to the campus area in July to begin to learn about the city and the university.

- He has a history of fundraising, including the creation of a $16.8 million endowment for the West Northeastern University Department of Journalism. The endowment created a nationwide news service staffed entirely by students and overseen by professors, making it the first of its kind.

STATEMENT FROM BURT SOSA, PROFESSOR OF ENGLISH AND SEARCH CHAIR:

"We had so many great candidates but Jim really came to the top of the pile. He was someone who had the background we needed as a university leader and the energy we need to keep the university moving in a positive direction. He jumped off the page, so to speak, and was so much more than his resume dictated. He had so many great ideas as to how to help us go forward as a university and yet he respected who we are. So many other people ride in on a platform of change. They want to change everything before they even know anything about a university. Jim didn't do that. He saw so many great things we were already doing and looked at ways to support and improve them. He also saw greatness in our faculty and offered ways to get our professors and instructors additional resources. He saw our students and offered ways to give them more education for fewer dollars. I couldn't have asked for more in a chancellor."

STATEMENT FROM ELLA SDELI, SENIOR POLITICAL SCIENCE MAJOR AND HEAD OF STUDENT GOVERNMENT:

"I was fortunate enough to meet Dr. Newcastle when he visited campus and he struck me as a bright, energetic leader. I think he's got exactly what this university needs to push us forward into the future. In these times of budget tightening, his fundraising skills will be a definite asset. He knows that students are our most precious resource and that if we all work together to do better, we will make this university great. However, the best thing he has going for him, in my opinion, is that he's a people person. I think he will take the student perspective into account in every decision and in every way possible."

STATEMENT FROM PAUL FLIPPERTON, PRESIDENT, WEST NORTHEASTERN UNIVERSITY:

"I'm really sad that we will be losing Dr. Newcastle as our provost, not just because of how much he did for West Northeastern University, but also because how great he is as a person. When I got here in 2014, Jim was the first person to greet me. He was helpful and energetic. He really helped me get my feet under me and he really inspired me. That's what I'll remember most. His legacy on this campus will not be forgotten any time soon, thanks in large part to his fundraising efforts for the journalism endowment. The 'News of the World' project will serve as a great opportunity for our students for many years to come. That would not have been possible without Jim's efforts. I wish him well as chancellor and I hope he does extremely well for the students and faculty there."

ADVERTISING

REVIEW

1. What are five terms listed in the chapter that appear in many good definitions of advertising?

2. What is puffery and how can it be problematic in advertising?

3. Define a creative brief and explain how each of the three elements within one works.

4. Define an actual audience and a target audience.

5. What is the difference between an immediate-action item and a delayed-action item?

6. List the important issues the chapter outlines for measuring the outcome of an advertisement's effectiveness.

7. What is native advertising, and how does it work?

8. What is the difference between benefits and characteristics when it comes to advertising products or services?

WRITING EXERCISES

1. Select a print, web or broadcast advertisement and assess it on the basis of the terms associated with advertising that are listed in the chapter. (If you make sure to pick an ad and not a public service announcement, the idea of "paid communication" can be assumed.) How well does it do in identifying the sponsor, providing information plus persuasion, delivering the information to a target audience and promoting its good, service or idea? Write a short essay that outlines your findings.

2. Hometown Fresh, a locally owned grocery store, has been losing market share to big box stores and chain grocery businesses. The owner has hired you to build a campaign that will draw people to her store, where she prides herself on the ideas of local ownership, using locally sourced products and providing a pleasant shopping experience. On the basis of this information and some basic research you conduct about grocery-shopping behavior, construct a simple three-step creative brief for the owner of this store. Be sure to clearly state what you hope to accomplish with the ad campaign according to this brief.

3. Find an example of an advertisement that you feel failed as a result of poor tone or its failure to jibe with the item's brand identity. What did the ad do or fail to do that made it problematic? Was there any fallout or backlash as a result of this advertising's approach that you can find online? What would you do differently with this advertisement to improve its likelihood of success?

4. Find an example of native advertising on a website you frequently visit. Briefly describe the advertising, including the source of the advertising, the specific product, service or

idea being presented and the goal of the advertisement in terms of action (immediate action or delayed action). Then, analyze the native advertisement itself. How well did the advertising do at blending into the other content on the site? How well did it do in terms of providing interesting content that still had an advertising-centric purpose to it? What do you think made it successful or unsuccessful, and what might you have done differently? Write a short essay on your findings.

5. Select a product that you think might interest people within your demographic segment, and analyze an advertisement for it in terms of benefits and characteristics. Create a list of each one and see how well the benefits and characteristics pair up. If you find an imbalance in the two, explain how you would fill in the missing element, be it a benefit or characteristic. Overall, do you see a pattern or trend in terms of the benefits and characteristics in the advertisement you have selected? For example, do they tend to focus on something like the product being environmentally friendly or the service making life easier on you? Write a short analysis piece that explains your findings.

MARKETING

REVIEW

1. What are branding and campaigns? What do they do, and how do they work together?

2. What are some of the tools mentioned in the chapter that marketers use to communicate with audience members?

3. What is a word bank? What is a brand dictionary? How do these items help marketers in effectively communicating with their audiences?

4. How do adaptors and innovators differ in terms of marketing?

5. What is strategic relevance, and how does it apply to writing marketing copy?

WRITING EXERCISES

1. Select a product that you use and locate as much promotional material on that product as you can. What are some of the campaigns the organization is running to sell this item? What are the specific elements of the product that each campaign is attempting to highlight? How do these campaigns fit within and reinforce the product or the company's brand identity?

2. Find a brochure on a product or service that interests you and analyze the content within it. Describe the overall theme of the brochure in terms of what it is attempting to convey to its audience. Who do you think the target audience is for this brochure? Analyze the various panels within the brochure. Do they all focus on the same thing, or does each panel tell a different part of an interlocking story? What types of storytelling elements does the brochure use to reinforce the theme (photos, graphics, headlines, body copy etc.)? What is the call to action associated with this brochure, and how does the brochure enable you to take that action? Write a short essay on your findings.

3. Analyze several advertisements or other promotional material from an organization for words you think might be part of that brand's word bank. What are the words you find most often repeated? What themes are conveyed and reinforced on the basis of your understanding of these terms in relation to the product? Do you find that the collection of material you gathered has a common theme and consistent message, or do you think it lacks a coherent marketing strategy? Justify your answer.

4. Apply the concept of strategic relevance to any marketing material you have collected for any of these exercises. (If you prefer, however, you can pick a new piece of material for this assignment.) How does the use of creativity enhance or undermine the strategic relevance of the content? How does the approach this piece takes enforce the value of the content?

5. Select a product, a service or an idea you value and do some research on it as well as the company responsible for its creation. Also, come up with a rough written sketch of who you think the target audience of this item would be. On the basis of the information you have gathered, write a rough draft of an approach you would take to creating an advertisement or an advertising campaign for this product. Begin by outlining the five levels of the creative pyramid, and apply each one to your product and your approach to the content you plan to create. Then, weave in specific aspects of strategic relevance and terms you believe to be representative of what you might find in that organization's word bank. Determine which tools you think would be most effective in reaching your audience with this content. Finally, craft a message that you think would be effective in promoting this item to that audience. Complete the assignment, and then write a short reflection essay on the basis of your experiences.

ANSWER KEY

CHAPTER 1 AUDIENCE-CENTRIC JOURNALISM

1. What is an audience-centric approach to media? How is it similar to and different from previous approaches media outlets took with regard to publishing content?

   It puts the audience at the forefront of every decision; it focuses on things that matter most to the readers instead of focusing on what the writer most wants to say; it disseminates content on platforms and in ways that best appeal to the audience. Answers will vary in similarities and differences.

2. What are three types of information media professionals need to gather to create audience segmentation? Define and differentiate among these three forms of information.

   Demographic information includes measurable items like age and education as well as check-box items such as gender and race. Psychographic information includes personality traits, values and interests, such as interest in sports, the importance one places on local politics and the views people have on issues like gun control or abortion. Geographic information relates to where something happens, with the idea that people are more interested in things happening near them or in areas in which they have a direct attachment.

3. What is the difference between a "platform" and an "outlet"?

   A platform is the physical manifestation of where the content exists, such as a website or a newspaper. An outlet is the media operation behind all of the content that goes out to multiple platforms, such as ESPN or CBS.

4. What does it mean to "personify" an audience? How does it work and how does it benefit you as a media writer?

   Personification is a way to view an audience by creating a prototypical audience member who embodies the most prevalent demographic, psychographic and geographic elements of the entire group. This approach to understanding an audience can help a media professional better reflect on what the audience wants and needs from that person's writing.

5. What do the letters in the acronym "FOCII" stand for, and what does "FOCII" mean overall as a concept?

   Fame, oddity, conflict, immediacy and impact. These are the interest elements media writers can emphasize in their stories to appeal to audience members.

6. What are the two key questions the book tells you to ask of yourself to ensure you are approaching your work in an audience-centric way?

"What do my readers want from me?" and "How do my readers want the information?"

CHAPTER 2 BEING ACCURATE, RELYING ON THE FACTS

1. What does the term "gatekeeping" mean, and how does it relate to the role of media professionals?

Gatekeeping is a content-selection process that helps determine what information the general public gets to see. Media professionals are occasionally referred to as "gatekeepers," meaning that they choose what information is published and what information is not. Years ago, media professionals could limit what people saw because of the small number of media outlets. Now, thanks to the internet and social media, people can reach the public without having to go through these outlets. Still, media practitioners remain valuable as both content providers and tour guides for the reams of other content available.

2. List some of the ways in which "fake news" can be defined. What are some ways you can avoid getting faked out when it comes to potentially false content?

Fake news can include satire, partisan news that slants toward a viewpoint, internet hoaxes and information that runs contrary to a person's own sense of value. Ways to avoid being faked out include examining the source of the material, looking for other sources that confirm information and clicking on links to find the information's source material.

3. What are some of the processes you should conduct in a basic fact check?

Check spelling of all words, examine proper nouns for proper and consistent spelling, review the math for any simple statistics, use a map to verify addresses or other geographic elements.

4. What is the difference between a primary and a secondary source?

A primary source is someone or something that was present for whatever it is you are researching. These sources can include a person who witnessed a shooting, the original text of a speech or a video of a news conference. Secondary sources retell or interpret what the primary sources provided them. Wikipedia, a magazine article and a person who is telling you a story he or she heard from a friend are all examples of secondary sources.

5. What does the line "If your mother says she loves you, go check it out" mean in the context of fact checking?

Don't assume something is true, even if it seems like it would be obvious. Make sure something is factually accurate by verifying it with additional trusted sources.

WRITING EXERCISES

1. Below is a list of 10 "facts" that might or might not be true. Determine if they are true or false through research, and include a source for each fact. If you find it to be false, explain why this is the case and cite your source.

   a. **False. Nixon was never impeached.**

   b. **False. Pencil tips are graphite and have been for centuries. Lead poisoning could have come from the paint on the pencils if the children chewed on them.**

   c. **False. The analogy was part of testimony regarding depression, but the press muddled the issue and developed the term.**

   d. **True. It happened in Des Moines, Iowa, on Jan. 20, 1982.**

   e. **False. Bulls are colorblind. It is the motion of the capes that annoys them.**

   f. **False. The Green Bay Packers have 13 NFL titles, many of them in the pre–Super Bowl era.**

   g. **False. This was a myth started during World War II, although the vitamin A in them is helpful in maintaining normal vision.**

   h. **False. Martina Navratilova has nine.**

   i. **False. The maximum speed a penny can reach is 50 mph, not enough to crush a head or kill a person. It will sting, however.**

   j. **False. Moore fired at him, but he was not actually shot.**

2. Conduct a "basic fact check" on the following sentences, examining them for spelling, numerical issues and other minor glitches.

   a. **United States, NW**

   b. **Neil, Antonin, 2016**

   c. **Marisa, Oscar/Academy Award, Best Supporting Actress**

   d. **Monet's, Giverny**

   e. **Pittsburgh, Daryle, May 26, 4 for 5**

CHAPTER 3 GRAMMAR, STYLE AND LANGUAGE BASICS

1. According to the chapter, what are some important reasons grammar and style matter to you as a writer and your audience as readers?

   Enhanced trust between writer and reader; improved understanding of content; consistency helps readers; more tools in your toolbox.

2. What elements make up the "holy trinity" of a sentence?

   Noun, verb, object.

3. What are the benefits of active-voice structure?

    It is clearer than passive voice; it strengthens your sentence.

4. What is one way to find grammar or structural errors in your sentences, even if you aren't a grammar expert?

    Read your work aloud.

5. What is one way you can tell that your work has too many prepositional phrases?

    It has a singsong cadence.

6. What is an antecedent, and how does it relate to pronouns?

    An antecedent is a noun that a pronoun refers to or replaces within a sentence.

7. Name two important things to examine in the relationship between antecedents and pronouns.

    Each pronoun needs an antecedent; the antecedent and the pronoun must agree, so that singular nouns get singular pronouns and plural nouns get plural pronouns.

8. What is a good way to avoid awkward construction or problems with antecedent-pronoun agreement caused by the lack of a gender-neutral pronoun?

    Pluralize the noun to match a gender-neutral plural pronoun.

WRITING EXERCISES

1. The sentences below contain at least one AP style error each. Locate the errors and make the appropriate corrections.

    a. **the Rev., one-third, in the pulpit**

    b. **Professor, 4, Ash, Blvd., Ohio**

    c. **Sen., War, three, Purple Hearts, one, Bronze Star, one, Silver Star**

    d. **1980s, South, Street, two-bedroom**

    e. **9 p.m., "Deadpool," delete Mr.**

    f. **16, dad, AAA**

    g. **College, two-room, $1,000**

    h. **F's, faze**

    i. **governor, Capitol, half-staff**

    j. **bachelor's, journalism, New York, magazine**

    k. **senator, Wisconsin, 2-to-1**

    l. **World War, II, Sgt., toward**

    m. **3, no hyphens, daycare, summer**

    n. **Interstate 94 or Interstate Highway 94, mph**

    o. **Aug., 6-pound, 4-ounce**

    p. **Eve, "Star Wars"**

    q. **Chancellor, yearlong, $5**

    r. **the Rev., St., Church, upgrade, priest**

    s. **Navy, 7th, Fleet**

    t. **"Satisfaction," No. 1, '60s, or 1960s**

2. Select the word that best completes each sentence.

    a. **she**

    b. **him**

    c. **them**

    d. **its**

    e. **their**

    f. **his**

    g. **its**

    h. **him, me, he, I**

3. Select the word that properly completes the sentence.

    a. **Among**

    b. **definitely**

    c. **lose**

    d. **wracked**

    e. **reeked**

    f. **break**

    g. **reel**

    h. **moot**

    i. **plane, hangar**

    j. **envelope**

    k. **altar, invoked**

    l. **aisle**

    m. **troupe**

    n. **cited**

    o. **flair**

4. Label each sentence as being written in active or passive voice:

    a. **Active**

    b. **Passive**

    c. **Active**

    d. **Active**

    e. **Passive**

    f. **Passive**

    g. **Active**

    h. **Active**

    i. **Passive**

    j. **Active**

    k. **Passive**

    l. **Passive**

CHAPTER 4 BASIC WRITING

1. What are the Killer "Be's" of good writing?

    Be right, be tight, be clear, be active, be smooth, be quick.

2. How should you order information in your story if you are using the inverted-pyramid format?

    In descending order of importance: from the most important information to the least important information.

3. List the 5W's and 1H.

    Who, what, when, where, why and how.

4. How does the chapter suggest that you should build a sentence?

    From a core of "who did what to whom" outward to less important elements.

5. How long should a lead be in a standard inverted-pyramid piece of writing?

    25–35 words.

6. Define and differentiate between a name-recognition lead and an interesting-action lead.

    A name-recognition lead relies on the element of fame to draw people's attention to a story. An interesting-action lead works better when the "what" matters more than the "who" in a story.

7. When writing an event lead, what should your lead include, and what should it not include?

    It should avoid telling your readers that the event happened and instead tell them what happened at the event.

8. What is the purpose of a second-day lead?

    It allows you to update your readers on an ongoing event by focusing on the newest information in the lead.

9. List the four types of problematic leads listed in the chapter.

   You leads, quote leads, question leads, imagine leads.

10. According to the book, how long should most of your paragraphs be in a standard inverted-pyramid story?

    One sentence per paragraph.

CHAPTER 5 INTERVIEWING

1. Before you interview a subject, you need to conduct research on that person. Name several places the chapter states you could find background information on your subject.

   Newspaper files, company websites, trade press, social media, other people.

2. What are the pros and cons of an email interview? When should you use them and when should you avoid them?

   Pros: quick access for simple answers, readymade transcripts and sources often like this approach. Cons: weaker reporting opportunities, and you don't bond with your source. Use email interviews when you have no other options or you just need simple answers. Avoid them when you need a deeper, broader interview or when you need to establish trust with a source.

3. When you contact someone to set up an interview, what should you tell this person?

   Who you are, what your story is about, why you think the person has value as a source, what your deadline is and how much time you will need for the interview.

4. What is a loaded question, and why is it bad?

   A loaded question is one that includes assumptions or statements that unfairly limit a source's responses.

5. What is the primary difference between an open-ended question and a closed-ended question?

   Closed-ended questions lead to simple yes/no or multiple-choice answers. They tend to be questions about the "who, what, where and when" aspects of a story. Open-ended questions seek longer, more elaborative answers. They tend to be questions about the "how" and "why" aspects of a story.

6. According to the book, about how many prepared questions should you have for standard news interview?

   4–5.

7. What is the best way to make sure you can record your interview on audio or video equipment?

   Ask the source in advance if this is acceptable.

8. What are two ways you can encourage your source to elaborate on a topic without asking another question?

   Through silence and nonverbal cues.

9. What are two good questions to ask a source once you are done with your main set of questions?

    Did I miss anything important? Could you suggest other people as sources?

CHAPTER 6 WRITING ON THE WEB

1. What is one of the biggest challenges associated with writing on the web, and why is it a challenge?

    You lack the restrictions associated with traditional media outlets, such as time limits and space limits. This is a challenge because it means you must place restrictions on yourself and keep your audience in mind at all times.

2. What is "shovelware," and why is it bad?

    It is the process of treating a website like a storage bin for content that has been "shoveled" from traditional platforms onto the web. This approach to web use fails to take into account the ways in which web readers and traditional-media users consume content differently or the differences in how the platforms can present content.

3. Name three things you can do that will make your content more valuable on the web.

    Tell the story with multiple elements, write in easy-to-use pieces and offer constant updates to your readers.

4. What is a blog?

    "Blog" is a shortened version of "web log." A blog involves a storytelling approach that uses short posts and bits of information logged on a website in reverse chronological order.

5. What are some of the benefits to blogging for news? For promotional areas like PR, advertising and marketing?

    The benefits to news blogging include the ability to provide additional content to your readers without additional cost, to take advantage of niche areas outside of standard "beat" coverage, to sidestep the mainstream media and to gather data on your readers so you can better understand your audience. The benefits to promotional blogging include the ability to humanize your organization in the eyes of your audience, to drive additional traffic to your website, to establish yourself as a thought leader in your field and to retain your focus when it comes to the organization's overall purpose.

6. What does the chapter mean when it states that you need to "establish a tone" on your blog?

    It means that you need to understand the language, approach and style your audience expects of you and then blog according to those principles. This will help you develop a specific feel on the blog and also help you establish a stronger rapport with your readers.

7. How can you use linking to augment your blog and serve your audience?

    Links can provide definitions to unfamiliar terms, give your readers background on your organization or the topic of your piece and provide access to original source material.

CHAPTER 7 SOCIAL MEDIA

1. Define social media. What are some of the key characteristics associated with it?

   Digital information-sharing tools and approaches that allow people to gain information according to their interests from a variety of sources. Key characteristics include that social media operates in a many-to-many model, it requires receivers to convey trust and authority on the basis of their experiences with the senders and it allows readers to pick and choose specific individual accounts to follow as opposed to relying on a monolithic media outlet.

2. What does the term "viral" mean, and how can the viral nature of social media be both good and bad for users?

   Viral content is material that spreads rapidly through multiple senders to multiple receivers of social media and then is quickly reshared by those receivers to their followers. This can be good if you are attempting to spread news quickly or to have your message gain prominence on a social media platform. It can be bad if people are sharing a mistake you made or a piece of content that shows you in an unflattering light.

3. A tweet should have what at its core?

   A solid noun-verb construction that focuses on the key aspect of the message you want to send.

4. What are some benefits of placing content on social networking sites like Facebook and LinkedIn?

   You have access to a large audience with a specific set of interests. You can use a link in your post to draw readers to your website. You can find opinion leaders and experts in the field who can provide you with feedback and other potential audiences that might have an interest in your content.

5. According to the chapter, what are some steps you can take to avoid creating a viral failure on a social media platform?

   Read from the perspective of a 12-year-old boy; don't barge in on a hashtag; don't let the robots run your social media without supervision; prepare for the worst.

6. The experts at IMPACT list a few tips that can help you build and maintain a social media audience. Name them.

   Pick your platform[s] wisely; let users know you are human; produce valuable content; consistently post at a comfortable rate.

7. What is the 70/20/10 rule, and how does it work?

   This is a guideline for posting content on social media. The rule states that 70 percent of your content should provide a direct benefit to your audience, 20 percent of your content should be "shared" from other sources and only 10 percent should outright promote you or your organization.

CHAPTER 8 LAW AND ETHICS

1. What are the freedoms delineated in the First Amendment to the Constitution?

   Press, speech, assembly, petition, religion.

2. List and define the three types of limitations placed on free speech that are outlined in the chapter.

   Categorical limitations: restrictions placed on freedom of expression germane to the content people wish to share. Threats, obscenity and false advertising are some categories of expression that courts have refused to protect. Medium-based limitations: restrictions placed on freedom of expression germane to the platform used to share information. The First Amendment guarantees freedom of the press, which traditionally translates to printed products. Other platforms, such as broadcast, receive less protection than do newspapers and magazines. Time-place-manner limitations: restrictions placed on freedom of expression germane to when, where and how people wish to express themselves.

3. According to the book, what is the difference between "free" press or speech and "consequence-free" press or speech?

   Free speech under the Constitution only means that the government cannot prevent you from publishing content or speaking out. It does not mean there will not be consequences for your actions, such as the private business you work for firing you as a result of your actions or someone suing you for libel.

4. Define libel and list the things the chapter notes are required of a plaintiff to bring a legitimate libel suit.

   Libel is a false published statement that damages a person's reputation. Libel requires identification [of the individual alleging libel], publication [dissemination of the information to someone other than the person alleging libel], falsity [the information must be provably untrue], defamation [association of the individual with illegal activities, negative personal conduct and/or illicit personal affairs], harm [damage to the person alleging libel] and fault [demonstration that the publisher did something or failed to do something that led to the libel].

5. What is the difference between actual and punitive damages in a libel suit?

   Actual damages are real losses an individual can demonstrate during a libel case while seeking financial restitution. If a libelous statement led to someone's being fired, that person can show a financial loss of salary and benefits, thus demonstrating actual damages. Punitive damages are financial penalties a court assesses to a libel defendant to punish the person or organization for acting irresponsibly.

6. List the defenses against libel outlined in the chapter. Which one do you find to be most effective and why?

   Truth, privilege and hyperbole/opinion. The most effective choice for the students will likely be truth, but answers may vary.

7. What is copyright and why is it important for media professionals?

    The exclusive legal right of people who create content to use the content or allow others to use it. This is important because it gives the creators of content legal recourse if people steal the material they produce and publish.

8. Compare and contrast fair use and creative commons work. Explain how each of these items can help media professionals avoid copyright infringement.

    Fair use is the right of media professionals to use some pieces of copyrighted material without the permission of the copyright holder for educational and information processes. Creative commons is a licensing option for intellectual property that allows content creators to dictate how others can use that content without forcing the users to obtain express permission from the creators. Both allow the use of some content without having to obtain permission for use directly from the creator. They differ because fair use pertains predominantly to educational or informational uses, while creative commons licensing has a much wider array of usage options that are set by the copyright owner. Other answers are acceptable.

9. What does the term "payola" mean, and how does it relate to media professionals in news and promotional fields?

    It is a term made popular in the 1950s, when on-air personalities took money to play certain songs. It now more generally refers to freebies and enticements people offer to media professionals in the hope of gaining favorable coverage. It relates to the two fields in that marketers and promotional organizations often want to offer quality opportunities to news journalists to assist the writers in covering things that matter to the promoters. The amount of free material provided, however, may seem like a "pay to play" agreement to some news writers, thus creating an ethical quandary. It is important for all individuals in the profession to understand the rules that govern each branch of media.

10. List the four steps noted in the chapter that help you work through an ethical dilemma.

    Assess the situation, identify the values, discuss the issue with others, pick a line and drive.

CHAPTER 9 REPORTING: THE BASICS AND BEYOND

1. List and explain the major types of events the chapter notes you might see in a reporting career.

    Breaking news: This comes from crimes and disasters that happen at random times and at any place within your coverage area. Speeches: A speech allows someone to talk to a general or specific audience for a set period of time on a topic that matters to both the speaker and the audience. Meetings: A meeting is an event where a governing body of representatives comes together to deal with the business pertaining to that group or the people it represents. News conferences: These events help a person or an organization disseminate a single message to multiple media outlets in a single moment.

2. What does it mean to "shell a story," what does a "shell" include and how does "shelling a story" benefit you as a reporter?

This term refers to typing up a basic set of elements in a story file ahead of time so that all you have to do is add the new material when you get it. Shell information can include some of the background you gathered, any quotes you got from sources before the event and optional lead elements, based on the outcome of the event. The benefit is that you don't have to write an entire story on deadline, because you have the basic material already set in your story.

3. What does it mean to "look outside the lines" at an event?

It means to look for things that are happening outside of the planned content of the event itself for potentially newsworthy information. This could include a protest outside a meeting, people introducing unplanned issues during a public forum portion of a meeting or an unexpected audience reaction to a speaker.

4. What is beat reporting and how does it work? Give an example of a thematic beat you would expect a local news outlet to cover frequently.

Beats are areas of specific news coverage that a specific reporter or team of reporters will cover exclusively. This approach allows the reporters on the beat to become more familiar with the sources and issues in that specific area and allows them to forge relationships with important people on that beat. Examples will vary: sports, crime, government, education etc.

5. What is a news peg, and what question does it answer about a feature story?

A news peg refers to the idea that you want to hang your story on a timely factor, much like you would hang a coat on a hook or a peg on a wall. The question is: "Why are you telling this story now?"

6. When you report for a profile, what are three things you should look for in terms of observation?

You should be able to describe the physical nature of the person as well as his or her essence. You should be able to describe the person's environment in terms of the things he or she enjoys or the things that surround this person. You should be able to describe how this person acts toward others and when he or she is more isolated.

7. List three things that will make for a good localization story.

A direct local tie to a topic, an indirect local tie to a topic or a topic that has a local impact but is also felt more broadly.

8. List three things that make for a bad localization story.

A big topic that has weak reactions because of lack of knowledge, a big topic that has no local impact and a bad topic that has no impact on anyone.

9. What is an obituary?

A profile story written about a person who died.

CHAPTER 10 WRITING FOR TRADITIONAL PRINT NEWS PRODUCTS

1. Explain the concept of objectivity and why it matters to news writers.

   Objectivity is a journalistic standard that requires news writers to avoid taking sides or infusing their opinions into stories. This matters because news writers are supposed to remain neutral in their work and present the sides of a story in a fair and impartial manner so that readers can decide for themselves how to feel about newsworthy topics.

2. List and define the three types of quotes outlined in this chapter.

   Direct quotes: information taken from a source in a word-for-word fashion, placed between quotation marks and attributed to that source. Indirect quotes: information taken from a source and boiled down to basic information and attributed to that source. This form of quoting is also known as paraphrase. Partial quotes: a mix of direct and indirect quoting in which a fragment of information is taken directly from a source and placed between quotation marks, with the rest of the information surrounding it written in paraphrase. This form of quoting is used to place emphasis on a specific element of a statement a source made.

3. What are the positive and negative aspects associated with altering direct quotes?

   On the positive side, you can improve clarity for your readers and be fairer to sources who don't have a complete grasp of the language. On the negative side, you can lose credibility if your version of a quote doesn't match what people can see and hear via digital media. In addition, you may inadvertently alter the meaning of the quote when you attempt to fix it.

4. What is an attribution, how does it work and what is the preferred verb of attribution?

   It is information included with a quote to help readers understand the source of the content. It works to help the readers understand who said the statement so they can determine how much credibility they wish to give the statement. The preferred verb of attribution is "said" because it is neutral and provable.

5. According to the chapter, what is the most grammatically correct structure for an attribution?

   Noun-verb, as in "he said" or "Johnson said."

6. Where does a bridge occur in an expanded inverted-pyramid story, and what are some examples of things that make for good bridges?

   The bridge is the second paragraph, where you decide how best to move your readers from the lead into the rest of the story. Examples of good bridges would include a direct quote that advances the story or a paragraph of information that cleans up any of the 5W's and 1H that weren't addressed in the lead.

7. What does the book suggest would make for a good closing paragraph?

   A look forward or an encapsulating quote.

WRITING EXERCISES

1. Review the following statements to determine if you think you would need to attribute the information to a source. Remember, you do not need to attribute material if the content is a statement of fact or something clearly observable. Opinions, however, require attribution.

   a. **No need to attribute**

   b. **Attribute**

   c. **No need to attribute**

   d. **No need to attribute**

   e. **Attribute**

   f. **Attribute**

   g. **Attribute**

   h. **No need to attribute**

   i. **Attribute**

CHAPTER 11 WRITING FOR BROADCAST

1. What does the abbreviation "KISS" mean, and how does it apply to broadcast writing?

   It stands for "Keep it short and simple" or "Keep it simple, stupid." It reminds broadcast writers to keep their writing short and simple to help the audience better understand their stories.

2. The chapter states that broadcast writing is done "for the ear." What does that mean, and how do you write in that fashion?

   It means that you should write copy so people can understand it when they hear it. You should write in short sentences, use common words and include words that have sounds built into them.

3. How does an inverted-pyramid lead differ from a broadcast lead? What is it about broadcast journalism that makes this difference necessary?

   A broadcast lead is akin to a headline in print, in that it gets the audience members' attention before giving them the important details. Broadcast journalism does this because viewers are often distracted or busy while the news is on, so the lead needs to grab their attention first and then proceed with the story.

4. What is a pronouncer, and how does it help a broadcaster?

   It is a phonetic explanation included in a broadcast script for words that appear difficult to say. It is meant to help reporters and anchors say a word properly.

5. What does the term "wallpaper" mean in a broadcast context? How can you write a script to avoid this problem?

   "Wallpaper" describes video that lacks storytelling value but is used to cover over the reporter's voice during a story. It can include random crowd shots or building

shots. You can avoid this by writing script copy that matches better with the video you have available.

6. What are the five broadcast story formats discussed in this chapter? Explain each of them in one or two sentences.

Reader: the simplest piece that has the broadcaster simply reading the copy to the audience without video. VO: stands for voice-over and has the journalist reading the copy while video pertaining to the story plays. VO/SOT: voice-over/sound on tape: This is an advanced version of the VO, in that it incorporates at least one soundbite. Package: a traditional news story that includes the reporter's voice, b-roll, soundbites and even a stand up. LOS: live on set: This is a package in which the reporter appears live to introduce the package and to answer questions the anchor asks after the package is done.

7. To finish polishing up your package, what does the chapter say are four things you should check before declaring that you are done with your work?

Check your time, check your pace, check your enunciation and check your pronunciation.

CHAPTER 12 PUBLIC RELATIONS

1. What are five terms listed in your chapter that appear in many good definitions of public relations?

Deliberate, prepared, well-performed, mutually beneficial and responsive.

2. Explain the purpose of a news release, and then list a few basic types of news releases.

The purpose of the news release is to inform the media about an important topic that deserves public attention. A news release, or press release as it is often called, can create awareness, draw attention or inspire action. Types of news releases include announcements, spot announcements, reaction releases, bad news and localizations.

3. Why is transparency important in public relations?

Transparency lays out all the issues associated with a topic, both good and bad. It is important because it enhances trust between the public relations practitioner and the audience, and hiding information only makes things worse for you and your organization.

4. What is the difference between an internal and an external audience?

External audiences exist outside of the public relations firm or the client's organization. Internal audiences are the people within an organization who need information about issues being discussed about the organization in public.

5. Why is it important to work with the news media as a public relations practitioner?

The news media can send your message to a much larger audience than you can alone. In addition, the news media can lend your message credibility by presenting it to that larger audience in their outlets.

CHAPTER 13 ADVERTISING

1. What are five terms listed in the chapter that appear in many good definitions of advertising?

   Paid communication; known sponsor; information plus persuasion; delivered to an audience; promotes products, services or ideas.

2. What is puffery and how can it be problematic in advertising?

   Puffery refers to the way in which media professionals can "puff up" the value of a product without relying on facts or in a way that cannot be objectively disproved. This is akin to hyperbole and is often viewed as legally protected speech, but it can be problematic if the advertiser goes too far and makes claims that lack substance.

3. Define a creative brief and explain how each of the three elements within one works.

   It is an organized document that pitches a creative marketing strategy to colleagues and/or clients. A simple, traditional brief includes an objective statement, support statements and a discussion of tone. The objective statement outlines what you are trying to accomplish. The support statement describes the evidence that shows why your approach to this idea makes sense. The tone statement [or brand] explains how you plan to give people the information in an acceptable fashion.

4. Define an actual audience and a target audience.

   The actual audience is the group of consumers who, despite an advertiser's intentions, actually attend to the advertising messages. An actual audience can be the exact group of people the advertiser intended or a group of people the advertiser did not initially consider to be potential consumers. A target audience is the specific group of consumers that ads will attempt to persuade.

5. What is the difference between an immediate-action item and a delayed-action item?

   Immediate-action items are products and services advertisers promote with the intention for the consumer to purchase the product right away. A television commercial for a sale this weekend at a used-car lot fits into this definition. Delayed-action items are products and services advertisers promote in a way that is meant to strengthen brand awareness, thus inspiring people to purchase a product from that company when they decide it is time to buy. A television ad promoting the overall quality of Ford automobiles fits into this definition.

6. List the important issues the chapter outlines for measuring the outcome of an advertisement's effectiveness.

   Be idealistic but be practical; set the bar at a challenging but reasonable level; establish a concrete benchmark; don't confuse measurements; establish a reasonable time frame.

7. What is native advertising, and how does it work?

   It is a form of online selling in which the promotional content is formatted to mirror the other content on the site, thus masking its nature. It works by using the storytelling tools and formatting conventions of news media to slip the content to audience members who might otherwise ignore it if they knew it was an advertisement.

8. What is the difference between benefits and characteristics when it comes to advertising products or services?

Benefits are the elements of a good or service that will enrich the life of a consumer. Characteristics are physical attributes, societal reputations and historical attachments that can be used in advertising to draw in consumers. The difference can be seen in this example: A new sports car has a 600-horsepower, V-8 engine. That is a characteristic of the car, but it doesn't tell me why I should care. The benefit is that the car can obtain speeds faster than any other sports car on the market today, which is why I care.

CHAPTER 14 MARKETING

1. What are branding and campaigns? What do they do, and how do they work together?

Branding is the process of creating identifying characteristics that come to mind when consumers think of an organization or its goods and services. A campaign is a series of promotional pieces, including but not limited to advertisements, public relations copy and marketing efforts, that promote a product or service. Campaigns fall under the overall brand identity of an organization but focus primarily on a specific aspect of something the organization is attempting to communicate to the public. While campaigns may last a few days or a few years, the brand identity is a long-term component of a company's marketing strategy.

2. What are some of the tools mentioned in the chapter that marketers use to communicate with audience members?

Email blasts, one-sheets and brochures.

3. What is a word bank? What is a brand dictionary? How do these items help marketers in effectively communicating with their audiences?

A word bank is a list of terms that should be used within copy to maintain the overall feel of the brand. A brand dictionary is a tool that organizations develop to define jargon in user-friendly terms. These tools help marketers translate company terminology into something that audience members can more easily understand. They also help maintain a consistent vocabulary among marketing materials that reinforces the tone and feel of the organization's brand.

4. How do adaptors and innovators differ in terms of marketing?

Adaptors are people who see what others have done and look for better ways to do it. Innovators are people who break the mold entirely and make revolutionary changes, as opposed to evolutionary ones.

5. What is strategic relevance, and how does it apply to writing marketing copy?

This is the requirement in advertising that the creative aspects of an advertisement relate to the product itself or to the overall marketing strategy. It applies to writing marketing copy because it prevents the writer from forgetting about the purpose of the ad and using creativity or special effects just for the sake of doing so.